CATHERINE McCANN

Diary of a Hippie

JOURNEYING THROUGH SURGERY

ELEONA BOOKS

First published 2001 by
ELEONA BOOKS
42 Donnybrook Manor
Dublin 4.

Ph/Fax 353 1 2838 711

ISBN 0-9531302-3-1

Cover by Bill Bolger

Printed in Ireland by
Colour Books Ltd., Dublin

About Catherine –

Her first profession, which she practiced for thirty six years in the public Health Services, was Physiotherapy. She now works as a Counsellor.

Catherine is author of four books. She facilitates workshops on topics such as *Living Creatively the 55-plus Years, Stress Management* and *What is Caring all About?*

She is a keen gardener and opens her Shekina Sculpture Garden in Co. Wicklow to the public on selected days in the summer. The garden has been shown on RTE, BBC and TnaG. It's also been presented on the Radio One series 'This Place Speaks to Me'.

She has co-led thirty pilgrimage groups to the the Holy Land over the past twenty years.

Recently she completed her MA in Theology.

Previous Works by Catherine McCann –

Who Cares? A Guide for all who Care for Others (Eleona Books 1997 2nd reprint)

Falling in Love with Life, An Understanding of Ageing (Eleona Books 1998 2nd reprint)

Time-Out in Shekina, The Value of Symbols in our Search for Meaning (Eleona Books 1998)

Shekina Sculpture Garden (Duchas, Government Publications 1997)

CONTENTS

Preface

When one is asked to write an introduction to the *Diary of a Hippie* and that volume turns out to be a typescript of a mere thirty-six pages, one is initially sceptical.... Not much of a hippie existence... thirty-six pages... what a sad life! But of course, this is no sixties 'trip' as the subtitle quickly indicates. It is an adventure into the (largely) unknown, in which we accompany Catherine McCann on her very personal journey. Any major surgery or serious illness is in the words of Seamus Heaney, a 'door into the dark'. There is naturally apprehension, the fear of the loss of mobility or independence. There is a real sense of crisis. For that reason, the *Diary of a Hippie* reaches out to a much wider readership than mere 'hippies'.

Crisis, however, creates opportunity. It opens avenues to discovery, to self-realisation and to a re-assessment of one's life and values. To attempt to travel those avenues in the form of a very personal diary is a brave venture. The diary is neither premeditated nor reflective. It is the NOW, the story as it unfolds with all its twists and turns. In *Diary of a Hippie* we accompany Catherine McCann on a quite remarkable journey, but then Catherine is a quite remarkable woman.

Catherine McCann came to my attention when I was preparing a radio series called *L Plus*, a positive guide to Ageing. Her book *Falling in Love with Life* was very much in tune with the tone of the series and Catherine became a key contributor. A further series on Retirement (*Is there Life After Work?*) grew out of *L Plus* and again Catherine was a core contributor. In between she also featured in her Shekina Sculpture Garden in the series *This Place Speaks to Me*. In all her radio contributions there was a great sense of *rootedness*. Hers was a reflective, commonsense approach which was grounded in Hope. The listeners' reaction to her contribution was very positive - here was someone willing to share wisdom which grew largely from her own life-experience.

This *Diary of a Hippie* follows that same approach. There is a wonderful sense of *unfolding*, as each day's achievement reveals the progress made and the boundaries reached. There is a marriage of the practical and the philosophical - the practical in simple advice on how to continue breakfast in bed while convalescing at home and on recognising the limitations (not yet!) of what one can actually achieve in convalescence; the philosophical in the reflection that came with rest in the Convalescent

Centre. One need only read the penultimate paragraph of the book to discern its key philosophy – LIVE IN THE NOW! It has been a therapy for me to read this diary, if only to realise how abysmally I have failed to 'live in the now'.

In journeying through this particular 'hippie's' diary the reader travels through all of the doubts, apprehensions, achievements, pains, discomforts, valleys and peaks associated with major surgery. What better metaphor for Life itself!

Catherine McCann is an engaging travel companion, but then she has already proved that in her Holy Land pilgrimages. In this particular instance, one senses that the journey is only beginning....

John Quinn
(Producer of RTE Radio programmes including The Open Mind)

Introduction

I booked six months beforehand the exact date of my hip operation but told no one. As the time of the operation approached I knew I wanted to make this event a real 'happening' in my life. My desire was to experience fully all that would take place both without and within myself during this time. I did not want simply to undergo, or endure the six week period surrounding the surgery in a passive way. My aim was to enter this experience with as heightened an awareness as possible. This included having an attitude of openness to what would occur - the ups and downs, as well as noticing the small details of what we normally see as the humdrum of human living like washing, eating, walking.

In other words I approached this event as an opportunity or in biblical terms as a 'kairos' moment. I realise I was fortunate not to be laden with anxious or fearful feelings either before or during the experience. I simply trusted the surgeon and his team and the process in general. That process included my trust in my own body's ability to heal.

I was also fortunate in being empowered with the knowledge I had as a physiotherapist. In particular I had worked for seven years in Cappagh Hospital precisely with patients who were having hip replacements. One could add though that such knowledge also makes you aware of the pitfalls and complications that can follow this or any type of surgery.

About a week before going to hospital when deciding what I would bring with me, my lap top suddenly came to mind! So in it went at the bottom of the bag. From day one I took it out and used it. As the days unfolded I began to see that writing down my daily reflections fed into heightening my awareness further and that this heightened awareness led in turn into what I wrote. In some way the creative part of myself wanted to express itself and writing seemed to be the natural way to allow this to happen.

As the days went on I felt maybe... maybe I might publish. I feel experiences and especially rich experiences are there to be shared with others in some way. Everything we do in life has an effect on others. Why then not share this time with people in a more open way? I have written before, sharing my experiences of working in the caring field and also about preparing people for life after work. In a third book I wrote on spirituality and finding satisfying levels of meaning in human living.

This is somewhat different in that it is more personal and therefore there is more risk involved. The question for me then was: am I prepared to take that risk? to share six weeks of my story with readers?

The answer I feel is yes. An ever-increasing number of people have this surgery each year and I offer this record of my personal experience in the hope that it might provide knowledge, encouragement and practical tips that could assist others who have similar, or indeed any form of hospitalisation, and indirectly their families and friends. My recounting of events as they unfolded contains various strands: straight medical details, personal thoughts and observations, religious/philosophical comments, and views on hospital and convalescent practice. This is simply the way the diary 'came out'; none of it was premeditated beforehand.

I am keenly aware that each person's experience will be different. The many factors which influence recovery include age, general health, fitness, and most importantly attitudes and expectations as one approaches surgery, as well as the occurrence of possible complications following the operation.

This diary which covers the first two weeks in hospital, the next two in a convalescent centre and the first two weeks at home, has been therapeutic for me personally. My stream of consciousness writing passages are obviously my own. I would encourage people to allow associations, memories, reading or TV programmes, visits from family and friends, or whatever it might be, become *alive* moments. Entering into the small happenings as they surface can make the overall *happening* of hospitalisation become an insightful and maybe even a joyfilled time.

My hip surgery became for me a source of personal renewal as well as giving me the invigoration that comes from a new hip - no more discomfort and the freedom of movement to do what I want - or almost, since it depends somewhat on our years!

Diary

STAGE ONE : HOSPITAL

Friday, November 24th '00

Room 431 - *my home* for the next two weeks. The view looks out on the Christmas lights of the nearby Shopping Centre. Standing at the window I can catch a glimpse of the sea and Howth. It is now five o'clock and darkness has descended. The room itself is amazingly spacious. I am extremely grateful to have a single room as I do not think my VHI - D plan – gives full cover for that. Hence getting it was a real bonus.

It is strange to be here at last. I have just read in my notes that I first went to see my surgeon in 1992. At the time the notes said I had been complaining of discomfort in my left hip for 4 – 5 years. So I have had this gamey hip for almost fourteen years! It has served me well, even in its roughened state. I hope the new one will last that length and longer! I have used a stick for the past eight years most times I go out, even if it is only to the end of the road. I am certain that this was what most enabled me to postpone surgery until now. It also allowed me to do everything I wanted to do until very recently.

I have a real difficulty in understanding other arthritic hip suffers who are reluctant to use a stick, (or even a long handled umbrella – often not out of place in our climate). I ask them to challenge themselves – why? Since this kind of problem is largely a mechanical one – a roughened head of femur and acetabular socket and diminished joint space – it can often be managed for years pre-surgery by simply halving the weight that goes on the hip. The simplest of all aids: a walking stick does the trick. Added to that of course is avoiding standing. This regime has made everything possible – including in my case heavy gardening. The eight weeks prior to surgery I did what I call my winter clean in my Shekina Sculpture Garden – a job that normally takes me from November to March to achieve. It was a relief to have completed that task before surgery.

I am serene and grateful as I start out on this experience. I truly want to enter and live this total hip-replacement event with de Mello type awareness. (A.de Mello was an Indian Jesuit and author of many books which offer exercises and stories, which he says 'are written not to instruct but to awaken'.) Awareness for him means living as fully as possible the now moment as well as adopting an attitude of openess towards the future. My mantra throughout will I hope be the lovely words of Psalm 16: 'I keep you Lord always before me./ With you at my right hand nothing can shake me'. Later the psalm also says 'in your presence is unbounded joy'. I desire to live more consciously in that joyful presence these days and to allow that loving presence be my support.

I arrived as planned at 12.30 and after admission details were taken I was told to go straight to the canteen for my lunch. Delicious food – my main course was lovely pink trout. I was told my baggage would be brought to my room. It was still at the desk when I came out from lunch so I took it myself to my room – one travel bag and three plastic bags with bits. I was like bag lady! I had packed over the last week with some care – taking what I thought I would need but with no extras. I started putting my things in place. No one seemed to notice or bother about me which was grand. But just before I went down to take part in all the afternoon's happenings a nurse spotted me and in seconds had slipped my hospital number on my wrist: number 291284.

Everything seems highly organised here. A group of five of us – all on the replacement list for Monday – three hips and two knees – were brought to the physiotherapy department and given a pre-operation lecture on the do's and don'ts of the immediate post-operative period. This took a while. Then off to the blood test section. This time the test was for blood clotting and matching. Then a surprise. I was ordered a lung cat scan! I have never had a scan in my life! Apparently my earlier pulmonary function tests showed a slight anomaly. Then to another scan in the hospital's new nuclear medicine department – a scan on the blood supply to my lungs. This is a routine pre-operative procedure for hip replacements in this hospital.

One nice thing I have noticed about the place here – the courtesy of staff. For instance when you have finished a test in one department, then that staff member personally accompanies you to the next department.

I had just concluded my last test to find Bridget, my sister, standing in the Nuclear Medicine Department waiting area. She then accompanied me back to 431. After only a few minutes a nurse came and formally admitted me by asking all the usual finer details about my health re medication, allergies etc. Pulse, temperature, blood pressure and oxygen saturation levels were all recorded by the marvellous new mechanical apparatus that fits on a slim trolley. A tip of a probe in the ear records temperature instantly. All these gadgets must cut down a great deal on nurses time.

After Bridget left I settled down to starting this diary. I do not know how it will go – I feel drawn to attempting to put words on some of what I experience. It may peter out – who knows. But at least I've begun!

The morning should, I sense, also enter this record of my first day – that time before I acquired the title, or status if you will, of patient. Am I now a patient? It all feels so odd. That bracelet around my wrist with my name, number, and date of birth on it tells me I am. Patient behaviour – I wonder what that is all about? We'll see. I must be myself, but realise that certain perimeters will be placed on me that I will no doubt find irksome.

The morning began by taking my dog Andy to the park at 7.45 a.m. At that early hour one enters through a gap in the park fence – well known to us regulars! It was good to be there with dawn breaking around me as Andy and I took our usual route around the playing fields. Then back for a shower. I was aware when – with some difficulty – I cut my toe nails, that that was a task I would not be doing for at least three months. Next to the hairdresser for a perm. She was mesmerized that I had left the hair to the morning I was going IN..... It is I suppose part of the three wing in me. I refer to the Enneagram, (an ancient instrument, whether Suffi or Christian based no one is clear, to assist people in their journey of self-discovery. It approaches the human personality through a nine-fold view of persons and focuses on our basic distortions or compulsions as a way of growing in self-knowledge. I have found it one of the best of the numerous types of workshops on offer in the area of personal development)

And then to a special time – Eucharist at home which included within it the Sacrament of Anointing. I felt very blessed and also strengthened by that celebration. I had then to leave immediately to be here in time. Leaving home was no great deal as I expect to be out tomorrow and Sunday for some hours.

Supper came and later to bed and my first night in the Hospital. An interruption – someone with the title clinical admission nurse came to ask me further questions as well as asking me to sign the operation consent form. It seemed like a job that would have been carried out by a junior doctor in my time working in hospitals.

Sunday, November 26th 6 p.m.

The Vigil! Yes it is truly the vigil day before my operation. A vigil is a time of waiting, getting ready. After thirteen years putting off this op, (my surgeon told me on my first visit to him that I would know when I was ready to have it – true), it is finally tomorrow... Supper was served after returning from my second days parole during which I turned on the TV. I switched to Songs of Praise to find Alad Jones presenting choirs from around the English speaking world singing from the Albert Hall. It was very beautiful and towards the end a Welsh soprano was added. She sang 'I'll walk with God, from this day on'. I dissolved in tears – tears of *profound* gratitude.

Since coming here I have been acutely aware of how blest I am having the best of surgeons, anaesthetists, nurses, household staff and others. Added to this is the comfort of the place – my large room (en suite), TV, phone by the bed, two arm chairs etc. Most of all is the great care delivered in such a courteous, warm, personal way. How could I not be grateful? Even the one irritant I have is a blessing. My room is situated opposite the kitchenette, so there is the chat of the staff coupled with the sound of the radio as they prepare the trays. Later comes the wash up with its inevitable clatter of dishes. After that it is quiet. Indeed it is mostly quiet here, both day and night, with the exception of meal times. I know I have a problem with noise – but this particular noise is in fact a blessing. How come?

The blessing of it all is that it tunes me into the patients in the public wards – some who may be very sick – who have to put up with constant noise, movement and other distractions all day and sometimes during the night as well. In a way I am almost ashamed at my luxurious environment – most certainly I am humbled by it all. I think especially of lovely Patsy who is at present totally confined to her basement flat in Sean McDermot St. She has lived though many, many stays in public wards and has had numerous surgical procedures, including replacements (not all successful) for her rheumatiod arthritis.

Back to filling in yesterday since I wrote nothing last night. Due to surgery being fixed for Monday morning patients need to be brought in for Friday afternoon to have all tests completed and to be brought through the various pre-operative procedures. With most of these completed I asked and was given parole to go home. All I had to do was to take a bath laced with Betadine Surgical scrub morning and evening. It is strange stuff. It makes the water very brown and has a strong smell of iodine. I don't think I have had a bath for three years or more. It seems though I won't be getting into my shower, (which means lifting one's leg over the edge of the bath) for about seven weeks after I go home. The sponge down method will have to suffice – with the odd friend washing my feet – very biblical. The betadine bath had Dead Sea after effects – it discoloured my jewellery!

After leaving here I went shopping to get a few stocks in for when I get home. An exhilarating walk with Andy in the Park. Muriel came at lunch time. She is my dog minder while I am here and is coming to live in my home. How profoundly grateful I am to her for such generosity. I hope she knows how much I appreciate what she is doing. Thanks too, to all you friends who are going to take Andy for his daily walks ... I know this makes a great difference in helping my recovery.

I went to bed fairly early, but had not slept by 1.0 a.m. (having not slept at all the previous night due to both hips playing up). Hence I decided for the first time in my life, after it was suggested by the nurse, to take a sleeping tablet: normison. I got four hours which was great.

Today worked similarly. The anaesthetist came early and took fairly detailed notes on my health as well as explaining the operation procedures. As he did he answered most of my written down questions. I requested having an epidural form of anaesthesia. I gather most people use that method now. It seems I may be getting more sedation during the operation than I had anticipated. Maybe that is necessary – I'll wait and see. I don't want to be brash yet I want to enter into the operation and what follows with the maximum level of awareness that is reasonable. After his visit I took myself off home for my second parole day but with strict instructions to be back mid-afternoon. I gave Andy two walks, one on arrival and the second in the afternoon. The unexpected took place at lunch. My microwave suddenly packed in! I knew it would be important to have one on my return home from hospital – it simplifies cooking so much. So my last task was to take myself off to purchase a new one!

I drove myself back to the Hospital and a busy time followed. My surgeon arrived. I was glad to see him at last. He had just seen my X-rays and asked me which hip I wanted done! The right, symptom-wise, is now as bad as the left – certainly at night time. However because of the poor weight transfer problems on the left and the length of time I have had that hip bothering me I said to go ahead with the left. He there and then marked the spot on my leg, not with an X, but with three large horizontal lines at the side of my thigh. I mentioned to him my two goals: first that I had my car outside to drive away from here (as he had previously told me I could) and secondly that if all went well I wanted to leave here on one stick. He hinted it might be a crutch. Anyway the verdict on that was that we would see how things went....

His visit was followed by the enema.... not too bad really. Some phone calls wishing me well, then a visit from Bridget which ended by her giving me a computer lesson! At 10.30 p.m. I was given tomorrow's breakfast! I have to fast from food and drink from midnight and will only be given sips of water all day tomorrow.

It is now 11.0 p.m. so it is time to close down the computer, have my iodine bath and then to bed. I forgot to say, that when I came back I was given the good news that I was first on the operation list. I am so grateful to the anaesthetist for arranging that. I hope it does not put out the others on the list. I felt I might be number three. It is tough on number five since they will be waiting until early afternoon.

Finally before retiring I placed my things in as accurate an order as I could for my confinement to bed for fifty hours. I tried to make sure that essentials would be within reaching distance on the top of my locker and also on my bed table trolley. I was particularly careful that my computer would be close at hand. The most suitable place is at the end of my bed trolley. This arrangement is obviously working or I would not be using my computer now. I did not really envisage I would be in form to operate it so soon.

So I am as ready as I can be. My mood is good, there is even an excitement there. I know I am in good hands, people are supporting me strongly, especially close friends, and the Lord is there behind it all – sheltering, supporting, comforting me with his Presence – yes his wonderful Shekina presence. Thank you Lord and goodnight to all and God bless all.

Monday, November 27th *Day One Patient* 7.0 p.m.

(Patients are known in this Hospital as day one, day five patients etc. This term refers to the number of days post-surgery)

November 27th has been a red letter day in my diary since last June when I went to see my surgeon regarding having my hip done in the Autumn. I had carefully planned in my mind for years that the timing of my operation would be November. My reason for that was it would come after the October/November Holy Land pilgrimage. This would also allow a sufficient period of time to recuperate before the March/April pilgrimage. Alas of course, the Autumn one did not take place this year because of the political situation. It is our first time over thirty-three visits to have to cancel. I feel so sad about what is happening to all the people in that land but I must add the Palestinians have my particular sympathy especially since my shocking visit to Gaza last year. However I do try to understand the particular predicaments each side finds themselves in.

Back to timing my hip operation. I knew too that May to August would not suit because of Shekina – my sculpture garden – which is open to the public on certain days over the summer. The Open and Time-out Days for 2001 are already arranged and have even gone to print in the Co. Wicklow Garden Festival booklet so that if I have to get my second hip done it will be this time next year. A little excitement I had two weeks ago was when my garden went on the world wide web! This has on it the dates for 2001, plus some details about the garden itself. I am delighted and proud to have this accomplished.

But back to the operation day itself. Since I was first on the list I was called at 6.0 a.m. I had slept four hours with the aid of a sleeping tablet plus also a piriton, (an anti-allergic drug) ordered as a pre-operative precaution by the anaethetist. To my surprise I had to have another bath with the usual solution – my fifth! The painting of the left leg and the shaving job came next and was simple and quick. Back to bed for the last set of routine observations, and then I was left alone to be quiet for just fifteen minutes. I took out psalm 16 and read it slowly and as prayerfully as I could. How wonderfully consoling that psalm has been over the past few weeks. I suggest to anyone who finds themselves in difficult situations to lean on this psalm and this includes during periods of hospitalisation.

Slightly earlier than anticipated I was whisked off in my bed to theatre.

A bevy of nurses and the anaesthetist surrounded me each one attending to different parts of my body. This seemed to take about five minutes and then I went to sleep.... not planned by me. I chided the anaesthetist about why this happened on his visit this evening and he chided back with a good answer: 'I didn't put you to sleep. You chose to go to sleep!' Maybe it was the lack of sleep over the past few months that finally caught up on me – aided of course by whatever sedative they gave me which again are strange substances to my system. He also said he found me very relaxed.

I was amazed to find myself in such good shape when I awoke in recovery. I was alert enough to ask to see my x-rays with the new hip in place. It looked just fine! (The actual prosthesis is a modification of the original Charnley hip.) No sensations in both legs of course, little pain, and no blood going in – just a simple saline drip. It turns out I may need no blood. It will depend on how much blood loss appears in my three drains. Another plus factor in this regard is that my haemoglobin was so good before the operation. No one can chide me any more about my unusual and often considered by friends insufficient eating habits. They are obviously OK. I am sure my odd gin and tonic plus a few glasses of wine a week also helps!

The day went fast. I recall phoning my sister around eleven to say I was back in my room alert and well. A good friend arrived after midday; there was little talking as well as some dozing during the visit. Bridget looked in at tea time for just ten minutes and I gave her a blow by blow account of everything.

I am aware it is Monday night and I know for sure that the prayer group is praying for me. I was one of the original four founder members of that group which started almost thirty years ago. To my delight I was well able to take out my computer and write up my operation day on the very day itself. Not bad going I feel, but it was effortless to do so. So far doing this has been good therapy for me. I plan to continue unless it turns into a chore. I watched Questions and Answers (imagine on the very day of my operation) and then to my astonishment at 11.15. my surgeon pays a visit. What hours he keeps – 7.30 starting in theatre and then late night calls to check on his patients – truly a remarkable person. He said everything about the operation was straight forward which was good news indeed. I felt that was the case anyway. Now it is time to settle down and turn off this machine. How thankful I am that I feel so well and know that everything went well also.

Tuesday, November 28th *Day Two Patient* 2.0 p.m.

During the night my obs. (ie. observations) were taken – I think two hourly. An antibiotic was started and is being given intravenously via the drip so there are no unecessary pricks. I gather I will receive one of these doses twice daily for two days. Just before settling down I was given a Volterol suppository (an anti-inflamatory plus pain killer) which can to be repeated every eighteen hours. My permission had to be given beforehand to the doctor to allow this to happen – because it is an invasive procedure? I thought of prisoners and how they smuggle drugs into prison by using their own bodies... The prison officers know this and can do nothing about it since it is an offense to be invasive in this manner without a person's permission.

I slept probably less than two hours but I felt relaxed throughout the night resting in a state of quiet contentment. This meant I started today in excellent form and feeling really, really well in myself. The first happening, even before the curtains were drawn back, was a blood test to check my haemoglobin and also my kidneys – I presume to see if there was no retention. (Haemaglobin is a very important constituent of our red blood cells since it attracts to itself the oxygen we breathe in and then carries this oxygen to all parts of the body.) I am on a light diet all day which means no roughage like brown bread or fruit or even fruit juices. I thought I would be delving into the wonderful choice of food from the general menu! I realise that this is all part of the careful attention to detail that manifests itself around everything that is done here. The light diet meant white toast at breakfast, consomme soup and ice-cream for lunch and I gather for supper it can be some form of egg, or a sandwich – again made with white bread.

I was in better talking form for the two visitors who came. It is now early afternoon so maybe I should take a bit of a rest and possibly even sleep? That would be great but I rarely, if ever, have managed to sleep in the day time throughout my life. At least I will close my eyes and that will be restful. Before that I must call for a bed pan. That was something I had never experienced until yesterday and was not looking forward to it. But even that was not bothersome. I fortunately have good biceps muscles which enable me to lift my bottom well off the bed on the monkey pole above it, and then a thin, pliable plastic pan is slipped in – a big improvement on the bulky, hard, cold stainless steel ones I used to see patients using. The other attachment I had removed this morning is my oxygen. I gather I only have to use it again tonight and then that is over.

A lot seems to have happened since lunch time yesterday hence the need to recall the remainder of yesterday's happenings first. After completing this diary writing I lay down for an hour and a half, mainly to take the pressure off my bottom from sitting up in the bed for so long and also to try and sleep. The latter never came but I rested my eyes and myself generally. That wonderful but elusive 'falling asleep' reality is eluding me these times. Not to worry – I don't feel over tired. I realised yesterday I was slightly euphoric. I am sure this state was the unconscious relief that the operation was over, but more likely, in my case, it was due to my feeling so well and so relaxed and able to enjoy everything as it unfolded.

Bridget called and brought in Maeve Binchy's book *Aches and Pains*. I am not sure whether to read it now – would it put me off my writing or would it help? I'll see. Maeve's style I am sure is hilarious although I hope my account is not without some humour. Muriel arrived a few minutes later. Not only does Muriel mind my dog but she also acts as my private secretary! Hence we went through my phone calls and post. It is good to be kept in touch with matters as they arise. One of the letters included my certificate saying I had passed my ECDL test! (European Computer Driving Licence). So I am supposed to be computer competent now. I am better at it, but still panic at times when the computer gets stuck, or I cannot get in or out of what I am looking for.

Darkness descends so early these afternoons and especially on a wet day like today. I had my tea of turkey sandwiches (again white bread. I normally never eat the stuff but I was so hungry almost anything would do!) I realise though just how right and well planned the diet for the first three post-operative days is worked out. Today I think is my last day on that fare. My hunger for something more substantial this evening is I am sure a good sign.

A few welcome and not too long phone calls came in and then the scene changed. On the last call I remember saying how well I felt but the period of possible complications lay ahead. I had no idea that was to follow within minutes. I started shivering and knew my temperature was rising. For the first time I felt unwell. I lay down, covered myself with extra blankets to get warm and then the next thing I was far too hot. My concern of course was what was the cause of the raised temperature – was it infection in my urine, chest, or worst of all in the wound? From that moment I attempted to tackle this problem by drinking loads of water and trying to relax. The temperature was 38.5 – not that high, but enough to make me not want to do anything. I had planned for an evening read of the *Irish Times* and had also marked out the TV programmes I would watch. That all fell by the board. The nurses were very kind because with all that drinking I needed the bed pan often as well as having damp sheets and nightie changed. The senior nurse was also very reassuring. She said the cause of the temperature was possibly environmental – a new one on me. She decided to not even give a panadol at this early stage.

Thank God the temperature came down to almost normal by 4.0 a.m. I knew it was around four because I received my last antibiotic shot at that time. After that injection the drip apparatus was all removed. At that stage I slipped off to sleep for a couple of hours and awakened feeling unbelievably better. Light breakfast was served and then the real action began. My drains were whipped out – not painful at all – and the oxygen was removed. So now I am free of all attachments! Something though was added – the elastic stockings which I know have to be worn from now on for several weeks. They are the one thing that I will be dependent on others to put on for me. They suggest changing and washing them every two days. Actually I am surprised at their comfort – so far.... They are much finer than the old ones I remember struggling to put on people.

Then after a wash two physiotherapists arrived for my first walk. I knew the actual walking would not be problematic. I wondered though would I be dizzy – not at all. So off I went on the frame. I could easily have walked the length of the corridor but of course the reins were put on me! I know I am not going to find this particular form of restraining easy. It was a great feeling to be out of bed and in the upright position again. I had absolutely *no* pain when walking. Then back to base again, meaning of course bed. What followed was a wonderful couple of hours of quiet.

The sun streamed into the room periodically flooding the place with wondrous shafts of light. Mainly the light focused on a huge bouquet of flowers which arrived last night from friends who were in Italy. I was very touched, that must have been arranged last September before they left Ireland. Again the kind thoughtfulness of friends comes home to me. How utterly spoilt I have been.

This turned out to be a precious time. Not only was the room flooded with light but inwardly I experienced being flooded/filled with a wondrous sense of joy and happiness. It is a long time since I felt my body and spirit combining together in such a unified sense of wellness. In my lectures on *Living Creatively the Last Third of Life* I stress what is meant by wellness and that it arises out of an integrated sense of our needs being met at the physical, intellectual, emotional and spiritual levels of our being. Now I was truly experiencing this at a deep level for myself. It was a good place to be. It is this type of integration/ wholeness experience that leads to joy and contentment. I am aware such moments are a grace, a gift.

Those two hours became a glory-filled time – a Shekina-type experience. I try to describe a possible way of entering such an experience on my Shekina Website. The words of my psalm had enhanced meaning – especially the line 'in his presence is unbounded joy' (v.16) The reality of these words formed the backdrop, or as Bernard Lonergan would say 'the under-tow' of the whole experience. (I chose Bernard Lonergan, a Canadian philosopher/theologian, for my research MA thesis on 'Conversion' – showing that intellectual, moral and religious conversion are the way we come to religious faith).

Lunch was quite spectacular. It was really my first proper lunch since I came to the Hospital. First of all consommé soup was served on a tray. After just the right length of time another tray was produced carrying the main course. The dish was covered with a marvellous silver-domed cover. It reminded me of my two day visit to Cairo some fifteen years ago when I stayed in the Sheraton. Some Egyptian tour company was trying to woo us to bring groups to Egypt. The first evening we had dinner in the posh dinning room (a mistake we discovered later) where the tableware was magnificent (I can't remember the food). I recall so well the great silver coverings for the main dishes. Today made that memory very vivid. Another tray came later with desert and tea. My choice on today's menu was lemon sole. It was delicious. The cooks here are really good. Tasty food well presented and not too much of it plays an important part in the overall healing process.

A visitor and then time for my second walk – how short it seemed. When I was told to turn back I did so by making as big a circle as possible in order to extend the length of the walk!

More visitors – including my nephew who brought a lovely 'get-well' teddy. Brendan stayed on a short while after the others left. I so rarely see my nephews on their own so it was good to have a personal chat with him.

Two further visits – one from a physician who had previously done my general medical to see if I was fit for surgery. He explained that the lung cat scan he ordered last Friday was satisfactory. Not long after my anaesthetist looked in. He warned me that both my mood and physical health would be up and down following this mediumly serious kind of surgery. The extra endorphins released in my system in response to the shock of surgery primarily focus their activity on healing the traumatised area. As a result my general physiological as well as psychological health might become unstable at times. In other words he was warning me to expect certain swings in mood and in physical well-being. It was helpful to hear that.

I will close the computer down for the night as post-op day three draws near closure. The only new medical procedure was commencing on heparin to prevent blood clotting. It is given by the tiniest prick of a syringe into one's spare tyre! I will have this injection over the next seven days.

Thursday, December 30th *Day Four Patient* Feast of St. Andrew! 1 p.m.

Just finished lunch. I was wrong about the menu. I am on the light one for one more day. I did have a small bonus. I chose caramel custard for dessert. I smiled to myself and ate with relish its garnishing: half a strawberry! My de Mello attempts to take time masticating and tasting my food to the full led me to relish that special strawberry flavour. I have a passion for strawberries since I was a child and my birthday cake has always been made of strawberries. For me red wine and strawberries (not taken together) are *the* celebratory drink and food. As a result they both call for company/friendship.

I was aware last night of the great support I have received from friends – visits from those who are close, phone calls, cards (and I note the carefully chosen words or comments on each one), flowers, prayers and in particular those who are involved in Andy's daily walk rota. Friendship – if ever I did write another book I would like to take that topic. However not being a C.S. Lewis – I have his *Four Loves* in mind – I realize it would be a task beyond me even though the desire to do something in that area is there.

Now back to the medical report of *the patient* who is now quite at home and enjoying that role! I settled down a little earlier last night – 10.30 –

was comfortable most of the night but little sleep came. I know I got two hours but I imagine I dozed a bit throughout the night.

Eight o'clock this morning my surgeon came on his formal weekly round. There is no big retinue of personnel – not like during my days as a physiotherapist in Cappagh Hospital. There was simply the head nurse of the ward – male- so I can't call him sister! I must find out his correct title. Everyone seems pleased with my progress and most of all myself. Knowing that there would be no round until next Thursday, just one day before my discharge, I put in my 'spoke' to go on crutches over the weekend. The request was granted!

I had no blood post-operatively. It was just as well I was late in applying to give my own blood beforehand. There is no need either to write and thank a kind donor which is what I intended doing. I had a blood test early this morning and the results are already back – my haemoglobin has gone up to 10.2 – two points up since Tuesday which is good.

Progress on day four is marked by being allowed to walk to the toilet but only with help at hand. An example of attention to detail is that where possible beds are allocated so that those who have left hip replacements have toilets on that side of the bed and of course vica-versa. This means you do not have to walk right around the bed to get to the loo. It seems you are not allowed to get out of bed on your own for a few more days. The morning walk on the corridor was lengthened and the same is due this afternoon.

I settled down to my quiet time mid-morning when all the bustle – washing, bedmaking, room cleaning and walk was over. Again consolation filled my spirit. In other words I tasted, relished, was immersed in an experience of deep joy and peace. How grateful I am for this grace.

Another visitor. The ideal visitor in my estimation is the one who stays for just the appropriate length of time. What that time is I don't know. It depends on my relationship with the person who comes, how I am at that moment, the time of the day, if others are there, and most of all I think if it is not filled with chat. I do find that wearing, even at the best of times, but particularly in hospital. It must be a strain on me because if the visit is too long or too chatty my voice gets weak and it quite definitely becomes a real effort to talk.

8 p.m.

Wrote my diary for a while and then it was time for my after lunch walk. My anaesthetist visited yet again and the usual brief words of concern were uttered ending each time with a kind of punch line. Over the past few days he has been my wisdom figure. Today he warned me, a bit like yesterday but in different words, that after an operation like this one remains physiologically unbalanced for six weeks. I took note....

I had the privilege later of having a quiet Eucharist in my room which was lovely. We had the St. Andrew's feast day readings. People who have had hip surgery here are banned from going to the Oratory for Mass because the chairs there are unsuitable. I am spoilt, yet again, in having this possibility available to me.

Following that I suddenly realized I had to get my back rest down and lie flat. I had been sitting upright in bed from 8 a.m. until 3 p.m. It was obviously too long. My blood pressure had dropped. It is always low but at this point it was 99 over 53. I thought of my anaesthetist's words.... I learnt a lesson – be very sensitive and aware of these changes and act gently by doing whatever is required to restore the body's internal balance. It always amazes me how finely-tuned our bodies are physiologically.

Another area of imbalance at present is my heat controlling mechanism. Over the past ten years or more I know I can go from being too cold to becoming over heated in a short space of time. This fact has been accentuated after surgery. Often when I take a simple cup of tea I get uncomfortably hot and then take my jacket off. Alternatively I can cool down fast.

A small incident worth recording. I could not get a hackney cab for one of my visitors (the taxi strike was on). But the reception staff were incredibly kind and got my friend a cappuccino from the canteen while waiting. I cannot envisage many hospital reception staffs even thinking of such a thing.

I will now close my computer and have a 'do-nothing' evening. I have just started Shusaku Endo's novel *Deep River*. I rarely, if ever, have read a novel a second time. I enjoyed my first reading so much that I delved into it too quickly. Now I have the time to give it a leisurely read and look forward to doing just that. Endo died recently and is considered one of Japan's top novelists, being likened in ways to Graham Greene.

Friday, December 1st *Day Five Patient* 7 p.m.

I am here a week today. My routine seems to have evolved somewhat differently today – hence my later hour at these keys. Two happenings marked todays progress: I was allowed to sit out in a chair for just fifteen minutes in the morning and again in the afternoon. The second, which seems to have broken the rather rigid (but I must add generally wise) regime was to commence on crutches. I managed these with relative ease despite the walks being longer and extended to three in the day. The one great hip 'no, no' is that you are not allowed to get out of or into bed on your own at this stage. It is obvious to us hip-replacement people why that must be so in the first week. You quite simply don't have the power to lift the operated leg against gravity.

Going back a bit – the good news was that I got some sleep last night, about two periods of two hours each. It made such a difference, leaving me with greater fighting form to face the day. One of the things that this experience is teaching me is the harmony that lies at the core of our being. When we are vulnerable, such as during the early post-operative period, this harmony or lack of it is more noticeable. I have become over recent days much more conscious of the body and the *quality* of its functioning, for example, eating, digesting, then eliminating!; the delicious sensation (I deliberately use that adjective) following washing or being washed; of cleaning and flossing teeth, brushing hair etc. Added to that list is the lipstick and the jewellery! Yes, for me personally, things like that help on the feel-good factor which must in turn assist the healing process.

Coupled with noticing these ordinary human physical tasks lies the heightened awareness of my psychological self. The interelationship between physical and mental health is far more closely intertwoven than we normally give credence to. An indicator of reasonable psychological health is clearly shown in the quality of relating to people. Right now I am actutely aware of my relationships with the staff here. I note – without being over-judgemental with myself – there are those I immediately warm to, and others less so; those who give me confidence and those who are less good at boosting morale; those who come in with a smile compared with those who have a slightly dour or over precoccupied expression on their faces; those who are alert to what needs to be done without having to be asked and those you specifically have to say 'would you mind doing x.. for me please'

The tasks I need done for me, while simple and ordinary are numerous and constant, like when you want the window or door open or closed, the back of the bed heightened or lowered and importantly for me to have my computer lead close at hand. Once something is out of reach there is nothing you can do about it. Managing this difficulty requires noting ahead of time what you anticipate you will need when any member of staff – be they household, nurse or cleaner are next due to appear. This applies to visitors as well. Of crucial importance is having the locker and bed trolley in the right position in relation to the bed. No visitor I think ever left without being asked to do something!

This brings me to staff. I experience high morale as well as excellent team work among and between all levels of staff. Each category of staff has both men and women. I was delighted one of the early days this week to be served my dinner with great panache by a lovely young man. I am particularly delighted to see this good morale among nurses. This has not always been my experience during my career in the Health Services. There are several agency nurses here as well as the permanent ones. Keeping the ratio right between the two seems to me vital. The agencies seem to have a good organisational set up. Those who choose this method of working often do it because they may be studying or simply because they want to work part time. The system obviously suits such people and it also is beneficial to hospitals who are suffering from the present shortage of permanent nursing personnel.

Flexibility and openess to changing situations must be the way forward in all aspects of human living in this twenty-first century. Such an approach is particularly necessary as we get older and as many altered situations impinge on our lives. Such changes could be in health, financial status, in moving out of a life-long home, in having to give up favourite activities such as playing golf, driving the car, when losing relatives and friends through death. Not all is doom and gloom – unexpected and unthought of pleasant opportunities can also lie around the corner. Here am I back to my workshop material! It is strange that my fairly large input into the RTE Radio One series: *Is there life after work?* should be running while I am in here.

I have really gone off on tangents today! The day was good and I really am aware of and grateful for my daily progress. Odd moments of weakness and fatigue do however remind me of my patient status. I took a longer rest after lunch actually lying down. I did not want the previous days occurrence of feeling faint to happen again. It is amazing how each day I have had four visitors – just right, no one stayed too long and all were people I wanted to see. Thank you all.

Late last night a catastrophe occurred – my computer sat down! I had to talk to myself seriously to handle that stress. I have had this Toshiba laptop eight years which I am told is very old in computer terms. It simply got totally stuck with nothing moving. I left it on until midnight in the hopes some wizard might turn up among the night staff. No luck!. So just as I settled down I simply had to pull out the plug. My self-talk worked to some extent since I had the best nights sleep for some weeks – over four hours. This surely proved I had put my computer difficulty mentally to bed.

Friday, being a day five patient – you are supposed to try and get your bowels moving again! There was no urge by nightfall so I took a small dose of milpar. Around 4 a.m. there were stirrings! I got to the loo in time but found it quite a weakening experience and had to return to bed as fast as possible. I remembered my anaesthetist's words – we are physiologically unstable for a while post-surgery. This incident was proof of that. Anyway it was relief to 'go'.

Today, and certainly over the next week I'll chose my diet and in-between drinks with two things in mind. Firstly that I go for high calorie foods to promote healing as well as taking those that have better iron content, in order to 'up' my haemoglobin levels. Secondly I'll choose those that are likely to facilitate bowel action. For instance at lunch I had a large and very delicious bowl of fresh fruit salad – with fruits of many kinds. I have also put myself on prune juice for my mid-afternoon and late night drink. It is drinkable if taken in sips!

Mood-wise I think, it was the day I dipped most. The main reason I think was that my energy level were lower than before. This did not however prevent me doing my four walks today. I went as far as the lift and back each time which is longer than I have attempted up to now. I was assisted as always in getting in and out of the bed but was left to do the walks with no one in attendance. This built confidence. On day five you are allowed to sit out for longer periods, so I had both my lunch and dinner sitting in the chair. I found this an energising experience.

I intend to be strict with myself over the coming months in taking a full lie down after lunch each day. I did that today and felt the better of it. I then had my quiet hour, or prayer hour, you could say. This, for me, is hugely restorative. Today was not a time of exhilarating consolation, but rather was filled with a quieter quality of peace, gratitude and happiness.

I know it would take quite a while for my haemoglobin to get back to normal by diet alone so I enquired about taking iron tablets. It was agreed that would be a good idea and I started on them immediately. I feel good about that. Two visitors today – lower than usual but that was good on a day when energy was down.

My surgeon has just made his late evening call. We talked about computers not hips! It is time to settle down so I am going off the air in the hope that all these golden words can somehow be retrieved off this machine which has served me so well over eight years. It has written three books for me as well as a hundred and eighty page MA thesis which included over 500 footnotes!

Sunday, December 3rd *Day Seven Patient* First Sunday of Advent 11.0 p.m.

I have been aware yesterday and again today how momentous today is for those who follow the Christian calendar. Advent marks the beginning of the Liturgical Year so today is the first day, of the first year, of the 3rd millennium. No one seems to have noticed! I have not heard it mentioned by anyone but it is true. I wonder will people notice January lst which marks the beginning of the first day of the first civil year of a new millennium? I have come late in life to developing a sense of history. Growth in historical knowledge widens horizons and offers a keener sense of perspective on both the past and the present. History opens us to the context in which the drama of human living takes place. It plays a huge role in our efforts to understand human behaviour and this includes my own.

Today was a very full day as indeed most of the days have been. The new things today were having my first shower and getting into ordinary clothes. I also ventured down to Mass in the Oratory. I realized a bit of rule breaking was required so I cleared the possibility of this happening beforehand with my surgeon. I had been told on arrival by the chaplain that 'hips' are not allowed down to Mass since the chairs in the Oratory are not suitable for post-op hips. However when I did my run around the place the Friday I arrived I called into the prayer room and noticed there was a chair there just like the ones we sit out in our rooms. So...

The saying 'rules are made to be broken' is one I call on at times. I do it with I hope some sense of responsibility. That means ensuring that the risk taken is not unreasonable. Put another way it means not exposing myself or others to what could be unsafe. Do you turn left at a red light at 5.0 a.m. when there is no traffic to be seen? (and I might add no Gardai in sight either!). I am not sure whether it is the adventurous, playful, maybe stupid side of me, but I can get an impish delight in risk-taking. Obeying rules for rules sake, especially when they have become largely irrelevant is not something I buy into.

After Mass – visitors. Over the week I have found that half an hours visit is about right – and I am talking about people who are close friends. After thirty minutes I seem to flag. The tiredness still shows itself in my voice; it is simply not able for more. I took a siesta after lunch. I was fresh then to meet two more friends.

Monday, December 4th *Day Eight Patient* 9.30 a.m.

Today I am an 'eight day' patient. (How easily I use that word patient now.) Imagine this time last week I was actually down in theatre! I am thrilled and so grateful for my progress. The words of a modern translation of Mary's Magnificat come to mind: 'I consider myself a very fortunate woman'. I truly can 'own' that phrase as an apt way of expressing how I feel.

I am allowing myself now to look ahead to when I go home. I live on my own so I plan how I will manage carrying out the ordinary everyday tasks. I was determined this morning for instance to dress myself. It worked and naturally I am delighted. With the aid of the pick-up stick, which I purchased before coming in here, I was able to do the tricky manoeuvre of getting my operated leg through my underpants and trouser leg. It has given me enormous satisfaction to know I now can competently achieve this task. That is one operation off my list! Of course dressing the top half causes no problem. Getting out of clothes is also easy – I did that last night. You simply let your trousers drop on the floor and then step out of them! I wonder why most patients here do not dress until the day they go home. I intend dressing everyday from now on. I consider it therapeutic; a moving away from dependent illness behaviour.

I feel almost driven this morning to start early on my computer in order to put down some thoughts on one of the most profound articles I have ever read, 'Not one of our own' by Anonymous (*The Furrow* Dec. 'oo). I mean that sincerely. I have been touched to the core by it. My immediate reaction was and is to stand back in wondrous amazement at the man who anonymously shared such painful aspects of his life's journey with readers. I hope many, many people will read this article. It is for everyone – but particularly for all those in authority, those who work in any of the caring fields (all staff here should read it), and those who are concerned about values in modern soceity and how we create these values.

Most all it is an article which challenges our personal attitudes towards *outsiders*. A strong warning is given about how we, both as individuals and groups, should *not* almost instinctively, rush in to 'help' in the traditional sense. The writer points out poignantly how a more appropriate response is to try to respectfully *journey with* those who suffer – particularly the suffering of aloneness and helplessness which he says is the core experience of outsiders. If anything, those who in the main have the experience of living an insider type life, should be open to allowing outsiders reach out and assist them – a role reversal which people may be unaccustomed to. It is much harder to receive than to give. Learning the art of receiving is I feel the great art to learn particularly in the second half of life.

I am truly under the influence of this insightful piece of writing. I know when I see a film I can at times come out and be under its influence for hours or days – depending of course on the film. That happened to me recently when I saw the Jewish film, *Kadosh*. This film, made in Jerusalem, is about two married couples who live as strict orthodox Jews. It was stark, but how it challenged. As with most good films it left me with many unanswered questions.

I have never had that kind of experience regarding the written word until this morning. Thank you writer and yes you are a hero. I would call you a prophet also, a word you do not ascribe to yourself. All you said was so true. I could identify with so much of it and will read the article many times because there was so much in it. I have known about some of the realities you wrote about. That is hardly surprising since I worked as a physiotherapist in the caring field for thirty seven years and for the last eighteen years as a counsellor, which is now my present work. On top of that I have tried to reflect on what caring is all about – which is the subtitle of my book *Who Cares?* In the light of your article I realise I was often only rummaging around at the tip of the iceberg concerning the qualities required as we caringly relate to each other – be they spouse, partner, child, friend, client, 'outsider' etc.

Exposure to new environments, such as this hospital stay is for me, leads to different and unexpected kinds of discoveries. For instance yesterday I realized in a new way how European Ireland actually is now. What brought this to my attention is the variety of personnel that make up the household staff in particular. It is quite normal, to have my meal brought in by an Italian or Romanian girl, my drink by a Turkish young man, or my stockings changed and washed by a Spanish woman! I find this all delightful, as Sinead O'Connor also said when asked by Pat Kenny on a recent Late Late Show what she liked about Ireland since her recent move to live back in Dublin. What astonishes and puts me to shame is their good English. I had two golden opportunities earlier in life to learn French, spending three months in Paris and later Italian where I lived for three years in Rome. I ended up learning neither language.

9.30 p.m.
I have just heard myself on Radio One, the fifth programme in a series titled *Is there Life after Work?* I have given a series on interviews before on radio but I always find it impossible to be objective when you listen to yourself on the airwaves. I was reasonably pleased with parts of what I said – especially the bit on maturing love. The topic for tonight was 'Relationships'.

Today flew by. Each day seems to go quicker. I have not been bored for a minute. Late morning I walked to the tiny physiotherapy department which was furnished with just three pieces of apparatus as far as I could see – a couch, tilt-table and the simplest and cleverest ever modification of what was called in my physiotherapy training days – a Guthrie Smith. I was reminded of my days working in Cappagh Hospital over thirty years ago when a row of hip replacement patients would be brought on trolleys each day to do their sling work lying on couches under an overhead mesh. My treatment session this morning was a very modified form of what we did in the past. My leg was supported in two slings and then strung up on a single overhead bar. I was only allowed swing it out to the side (i.e. abduct) thirty times. This was followed by the simpler and for me more difficult exercise of trying to bed up at the hip and knee (flexion) One did this by sliding your heel along a board. The treatment was all over in five minutes!

I have always believed that physiotherapy following joint replacement surgery is very simple but none the less important for that. Apart from a few basic exercises it is as much about what you do *not* do as well as what you do. Breaking the wires or dislocation of the new hip are the dreaded complications. To prevent this happening the emphasis lies on ordinary activities such as: the correct way of getting in and out of bed and chair, on and off the toilet, in and out of the car, and how to do stairs, and learning to be confident in carrying out these manoeuvres. Stairs I start tomorrow and the car bit I attempt on Friday. For people with knee replacements the emphasis is on knee bending exercises.

This afternoon I possibly had too many visitors although I was happy and really wanted to see those who came. I found myself drooping for a short while, but recovered well after supper when I lay down for a while.

One small, but happy incident occurred this afternoon. One of the cleaners, Lisa, came in to do my room. I love her bright-eyed, perky approach as she enters the room with her cleaning trolley and vacuum cleaner. When she came to wiping the top of my trolley I warned her to be careful of my computer. Then I told her I was using it to write up my experience in this place. She was interested and became more so when I said I had mentioned how good all the staff were and that included the important work she was doing. She seemed very thrilled by my comment and went off to tell her colleague and later her supervisor!

It reinforced something I already know, namely the importance of giving encouragement and praise. We all thrive on it yet why do I/we fail so miserably in offering it? I shall remember with gratitude this incident and hope it has deepened my resolve to give encouragement in my everyday relating with others. It does not matter what a person's perceived status in life is; the street cleaner and the President equally need to be given genuine praise for who they are and what they do. We flourish when this happens – provided of course we can receive genuine compliments. Lisa did this and in such a lovely spontaneous way. That in turn made me feel good – so benefits all round!

I apply to the Lisa incident a quotation made by Mark Fitzgerald in last week's *Irish Times* Saturday magazine. Mark says: 'I heard a great line the other day: it's a vision issue- that is, the *ability to see the invisible*' (italics are mine). This quotation in turn links with something I read in the recent *Tablet* periodical. The writer was speaking about the French philosopher Simone Weil who died young in the middle of the last century. He said 'her contemplation was about *seeing the world in a different and truer perspective* and above all of *developing a sharp eye and ear for the traces of God in all human activity*. I would sincerely desire to have that contemplative spirit but I can honestly say my experience this past week and an incident such as the Lisa one described above are taking me further down that road.

Tuesday, 4th December   *Day Nine Patient*   8.0 p.m.

I went to bed singing last night. After closing down my computer I did my usual late night walk. It was almost midnight. As I turned around the final corner of the square route of corridors, I bumped into my surgeon again doing his late round of the patients he had operated on that day. I was fully dressed and walking quite well on the two crutches. His first words in jest were 'You look ready for home!' Then came a genuine exclamation 'that's tremendous.' I think he was very pleased and I received his praise with great joy. He then recalled my wish to be able to walk partially on one crutch when at home. So he took away my left crutch and said 'walk' which I duly did with ease, without putting too much weight on the operated leg.

When you live on your own it is imperative that at times you are able to walk safely with just one crutch – otherwise how, for instance, could you carry a pot of tea from a. to b. even over the shortest of distances? My spirits were not down, but that brief encounter left them soaring! One thing I have noticed about my surgeon, with whom I worked in Cappagh Hospital, and now as his patient, is his positivity and ability to encourage – just what I was talking about in my Lisa experience.

This morning was active but relatively uneventful. Shower, dressed myself, then walked to physiotherapy for sling exercises. The one new thing was doing the stairs. I knew they would be no problem and neither were they. By mid-morning I needed a rest so settled myself in the chair in the corner of the room where I can see Howth. Today there were white horses in Dublin Bay. I watched for the first time ever the traffic that steadily flows in and out from Dublin Port – many tankers and a few ferries.

It was a prayer-filled time. I have been relying on the psalms almost entirely over the past while as my springboard to coming into God's presence. Most people who read or pray the psalms are aware of the depth and range of human emotion that is contained throughout the psalter. What I have noticed this time – not too strangely – are the *references to the body*. For example: 'My heart exults, my soul rejoices/ *my body too will rest securely....*' (Ps.15:9); 'Instil some gladness and joy into me,/ *let the bones you have crushed rejoice again.*'!!! (Ps 51:8) How apt after hip replacement surgery! I think of my greater trochanter- a section of the top of the femur, which is sawed off by some surgeons during surgery (including my surgeon) to allow the implant section be put in place. This bit of bone is then wired back again. This takes three months to heal – like any fracture.

Two stanzas from the well-known psalm 139 (13-15) are particularly body-orientated:

> It was you who created my inmost self,
> and put me together in my mother's womb:
> for all these mysteries I thank you,
> for the wonder of myself, for the wonder of your works.
>
> You know me through and through,
> from having watched my bones take shape
> when I was being formed in secret,
> knitted together in the limbo of the womb.

Lovely.....

Christianity, that amazing – too-good-to-be-true religion – is based on the Incarnation. It is an intensely body-centred reality. We – us Christians I mean – will be celebrating Christmas soon – the greatest of all mysteries which proclaims: 'The Word *became flesh*. He came to live among us'. (Jn 1:14) None of the great world religions, or the two other monotheistic faiths – Judaism and Islam – can conceive of a God becoming one of us; of a God who enters human skin. Jesus – Emmanuel – which means God with us, is like us in all things (except sin), Paul tells us. In other words he became *fully human*. One of the main purposes of his human existence was to be the way, *the way that enables us* to become more human (both as individuals and as societies.) As I see it, Jesus shows, by his lifestyle, his code of living as exemplified particularly in the Beatitudes, and particularly by the values and attitudes he expressed in his personal relating, what the ingredients are that ensure our becoming fully alive as human people. For me, no philosophy, religion, or scientific approach to life, can offer anything as satisfying and truthful, concerning the marvel of our human spirit's existence, as can Jesus. The best way of tuning into or opening ourselves further to a greater knowing of him is to reflectively read the gospels. Coming in contact with those who are fired by the spirit of Jesus can also help.

I have spoken of gratitude before. The thing in life I am most grateful for is being gifted with belief in Jesus. I get sad at times when I see people – including family and friends – so turned off Christianity. This is understandable if the focus of the Christian way of life centres on church and not on Jesus. The church is a meaningless entity without Jesus. Centering on church is also limited if it dwells solely on the human, and particularly the negative aspect of being human, in regard to church. The focus in recent times has been almost entirely on weaknesses, limitations and gross injustices of differing kinds. This side of church can get so much in peoples way that the person of Jesus remains hidden. Recently it has become almost politically incorrect to speak of the Church's positive qualities such as being the bearer of truth, beauty and 'good news'; the compassionate servant who reaches out to the poor and needy; the prophet who promotes respect and care for the universe and equality and inclusivity for all people.

My own personal testimony is simple. The person of Jesus, the Spirit he gave us, and the Father he points us towards, are the energising force of my life. The God who is love, revealed to us in the person of Jesus, shares his own dynamic way of loving with us. This love of God is always on offer to everyone whether they realise it or not. Simon Weil, whom I quoted yesterday, hints that the normal way we come to know this love is through 'the traces of God' which are found largely in the quiet, ordinary experiences of our lives.

It is this *certain* knowing and as a consequence reliance on God's unconditional love that colours my living. Life without this personal knowing of an all loving and *forgiving* God would for me be both a colourless and rudderless way of life. The quiet knowing that I am loved, and that I am called in turn to love others in the way Jesus loved, is what urges me to do what I do, and to become more truly the person I am destined to be.

This hospital experience has offered me numerous 'traces of God' in the people I encounter, all the various happenings and in the small discoveries I make. One of the surest overall trace of God this past two weeks has been the abiding sense of joy and aliveness which has pervaded my being. It has come totally unexpectedly. A card I received from my sister in America had a lovely one line caption printed inside: 'Happy healing'!

How true in my case. I know this happiness can recede from this conscious level but I am enjoying and savouring it while it is present. Everything ultimately in life is gift. We cannot hold onto anything for certain – health, possessions, relationships, happiness.

I hope this 'outburst' does not sound 'preachy'. These words were written whilst experienceing a passionate appreciation of the marvels of the Christian Mystery and what that mystery means to me.

On a lighter note: talking about holding onto things, I have discovered a great secondary use of my crutches. At times I make them work for me like chop sticks when, for example, I want to pick something off the floor or even lift my foot into position such as on the foot rest. They are also great for pushing things away, like opening a door, or pulling things towards you. I am learning fast the many useful tricks these valued appendages can accomplish!

Before lunch I took my second walk and decided I would walk briefly outside the building and down the front steps. The breath of fresh air was a real reviver. The rest of the day was quieter. I had very few visits from staff as I do not need checking any more except night and morning. I also had less visitors. I think I needed that space. I do dip after lunch so I now realize my mid-afternoon rest needs to be extended to two hours at least. After supper I perk up again.

Closing time. I am slightly anxious about tomorrow when I become *Day 10 patient*. This is an important day when systems are checked: blood test, hip x-ray, and pulmonary scan have all to be done.

Wednesday, 6th December *Day Ten Patient* Budget Day! 1.30 p.m.

I am using my computer sitting out for the first time. I am finding sitting a bit easier every day.

This morning was busy as I had anticipated. My blood test was taken early after which I washed and dressed – all before breakfast came. Precisely at nine o'clock I was whisked down in a wheel chair to the Nuclear Medicine Department for my pulmonary scan. The purpose of this scan is the early detection of possible emboli formation in the lung. If these are spotted – and statistics show that the ratio for this happening is 8:1 for hip replacement patients – the treatment is to be put on warfarin (an anticoagulant) for three months. This would mean staying on here for three further days to get the warfarin levels right. I should add that not every hospital has the equipment to do this screening. For me it was a deciding factor in coming here. A consultant physician, reports on this test this evening so I will not know the results until the morning. Patience! Not my best virtue.

I next went to have my hip x-rayed and asked to see the film afterwards. To me it looked great! but again I must await the expert's report. My brief session in physiotherapy followed. As I walked back to my room I discovered myself naturally moving from three into two point gait. This is a quicker and more natural way of walking with crutches. However I could not keep this up as my unreplaced hip started making noises! It did not like this new method since it meant it had to bear more weight! I am in transition right now in the sense that I don't know which is my good and which is my bad hip! I also notice myself being taller which is in fact true. I will not benefit fully from this regained height until the second hip is done.

I am very aware these past two days – apart from the mid-afternoon tiredness – of how well I feel. It is as though all my systems are functioning better. I ask myself why? Is it: that I am taking more rest? am eating consistently better food and doing so in a much slower fashion? am generally very relaxed? am more conscious of the love and support that has been clearly expressed by my family and friends? or, that I am resting more appreciatively in God's love in a more heart-knowing way? It is probably due to a mixture of all these things.

My prayer time led me to reflect further on this heart-knowing way of experiencing God's love. A classic saying from that delightful book *The Little Prince* came to mind '*It is only with the heart that one can see rightly; what is essential is invisible to the eye.*' Echoes of a biblical passage which is read at midnight Mass at Christmas also seemed to sum up my experience well: 'The loving kindness of our God has appeared to us' (Tit.3:4). I have many times throughout each day here experienced the tender loving kindness of God appearing to me in a myriad of ways – through people, events, the stirrngs of my own heart.

This morning I was introduced to a new category of hospital personnel: the hospital assistant. Their brief is broad and interesting and includes, security, maintenance, night reception, and transferring patients from the wards to the various departments. At the moment the five assistants are all men and are dressed smartly with white shirts and ties. Each one carries a walkie-talkie. I was used to the role porter but this broader brief seems to me an excellent idea. Again – courtesy was what struck me in the way they related to me.

This leads me to another staff issue – the nurses. While I understand what happened today I was also taken aback. Since *Day 8* I have been practically independent so I don't need their care except to administer drugs and take daily observations. While I am happy to see that more time goes to those whose needs are greater I did not expect such a drastic reduction in human contact. I would have liked someone putting their head in the door periodically making comments such as 'how are you?' or 'are you alright?' Personal communication today must have be down to three minutes spread over four visits. My iron tablet was given out at breakfast. The next visit was to take my pulse, temperature etc. at 6.0 p.m. An hour later I received my heparin prick and late in the evening the night nurse will come with a pain-killer which helps me sleep.

I was also a bit disconcerted by the fact that when nurses go off duty for a day or two and come back they are allocated different patients. I realize from the nurses viewpoint that this changing of patients gives them variety. It also alerts them to what is going on in the entire ward. But from the *patient's perspective* I wonder... As I stand back and look at this arrangement I say maybe the lack of the ongoing interpersonal relating between nurse and patient (which has a therapeutic value in its own right) has to be sacrificed for the excellent high-tech care. This care is certainly delivered personally but the relationship ends after one or two days at most. I do not want to appear over critical. I simply note what is. I certainly have no answer to this difficulty.

I know that while I do not see nurses personally they are there in the background monitoring and recording everything on computer. The trouble is that it is so much at a distance....and there does seem to be a lot of time spent on recording – an over-proportionate length of time? I presume a lot of this is to cover possible legal implications at a later date.

If you ask for something and that includes information that is attended to. I suppose the Freedom of Information act comes into play. I wonder how much most patients are aware of this act and their right to be informed on all issues.

I have mentioned painkillers in passing. I have always been fascinated by people's different pain thresholds both in my professional work as well as among family and friends. It is impossible to measure pain. Pain is a subjective experience and so it differs for each person. Often if the pain is chronic, relief can come through better postural positioning, or the right balance of rest and exercise, or the right intake of food, or by distracting/pleasurable activities – in other words *without* taking drugs.

I personally have experienced little pain over the past two weeks and therefore have had little need for pain relief in the form of medication. While here I have had one cyclimorph injection two hours after I came back from theatre for back pain (the after effects of the epidural I suppose.) I then had two volterol suppositories (an anti-inflamatory as well as an analgesic) before settling to sleep the first two nights. Since then all I have had in the form of painkillers is distalgesic – a mild painreliever. I take one at night to make me as comfortable as possible so that I am more likely to sleep, and very occasionally one in the morning. Have I been lucky or what? I myself have always made a distinction between what I call discomfort and real pain.

Thursday, December 7th *Day Eleven Patient*   10.0 p.m.

Washed and dressed before breakfast – getting ready for the good news. It came at 8.0 a.m. when my surgeon came on his official round and said I am discharged tomorrow! Everything has gone so incredibly to plan right up to this point of discharge. A friend came before lunch and helped me pack some of my things away. How kind of her. I felt ready to go there and then but there is still almost a day to go. The only final job still to be done is to have the stitches out tomorrow.

After lunch the group of hip replacement people who came in two weeks ago were given our final pep talk by the physiotherapist. The rest of the day was relatively uneventful. A friend came for supper. We shared my meal together and opened a bottle of wine to celebrate. I had brought this in the night before my operation especially for this moment! Wine is medicinal and is particularly high in iron. Hence I particularly need it these times to build my haemoglobin which unfortunately has dropped three points. A very good excuse!

I have made many discoveries about myself and other realities during my stay. These discoveries have been in both the physical and psychological realms. An important one for me concerns the value of drinking plenty of water. Up to this I rarely drank water and here I was drinking at least four litres a day! I attribute the greater sense of wellness I have felt – despite the inevitable shock to the system that occurs through any form of surgery – in some measure to this increased input of fluid. I intend keeping up this new drinking habit – well not quite four litres.

As I look back over my time here I ask myself what were the key things I have learnt? More importantly what changes in lifestyle are required by these new insights? I can answer both questions by using an umberella phrase – *SLOW DOWN*. I have tended since childhood to rush at and through things; to pack a whole amount of action into each day, each week, each year. I do not have deep regrets about this because it meant living a very full life. But, and it is a very big but, how much have I really entered into and enjoyed the act of living itself? It's a sobering thought because one of the consequences of my kind of lifestyle is to have missed much. As Newman points out we can have a wide range of experiences but have missed the meaning that lies behind them. Imagine next Monday on Radio One I will be the almost sole contributor to the interview titled: *Enough to live on – Enough to live for?* It is all about the question of meaning and finding new meanings and new goals when we leave the work place.

Rush, routine, and deadlines, often mean living on the surface of things; not noticing the beauty of the world around me and more importantly the beauty in the hearts of the people I meet; a failing to de-familiarize the familiar. Part of the problem is not even knowing what I have missed!

Moving towards more meaning-filled living inevitably requires changing gear, living at a slower pace. This for example demands eating, driving the car, even reading and a whole host of other activities, in a slower fashion. Only then can I savour, take in, what I am actually at! The present moment contains more (richness) within it than I can ever have the capacity to hold. (This is a P.J. de Caussade idea. He was a French Jesuit who lived in the 17th century. The title of one of his books, *The Sacrament of the Present Moment* is a phrase that has held a very formative influence in my life for years.). I firmly believe in the great richness that is available to us in every moment of our lives if only we could become more aware of this. Now I have to enhance this reealisation further.

I'll settle down somewhat earlier tonight in order to begin facing the challenge of stage two of the recovering process. Tomorrow I finish being the patient and immediately enter a more elusive time – the period of convalescence. I wonder how that will go. We will see.

STAGE TWO: CONVALESCENCE

Friday, December 8th 9.0 p.m.

I rested after breakfast waiting for the nurse to take out my stitches. It was more tedious than I thought but not painful. The nurse took great care as she performed this task. The stitches were the old style stitched type as opposed to staples. The wound was in super condition – almost healed – so a very slim dressing was put back on it. Again I was grateful that there were no hitches at the last minute.

I took my time getting ready, which included final packing, saying good-bye to staff and some patients. I was ready for take-off! Many staff were surprised that I was driving myself off the premises. I was carefully seen into the car by a nurse and hospital attendant. The latter arrived up to the ward with a wheel chair. I said that was for the luggage!

I drove down the drive and off to the Convalescent Centre with no difficulty. I do have automatic gears so driving is not the problem. What requires care and attention is getting in and out of the car the correct way. Being small and light I suppose helps but then my car is a small model. The journey to the Centre took no time. As I drove in front of the building and parked I saw no one around so I decided to get out of the car myself. I knew the procedure and took my time at it. It is something I'll have to do on my own so I said now is the time to start. It worked.

Somewhat late I went straight to lunch in the dinning room. After that I met a sister who kindly offered to give me communion if I wanted. I accepted gladly especially being a feast day. Being fed like this in both body and soul was I sensed a good way to commence my time here. I was shown to my room and formal admission procedures were gone through and then a most welcome visit from the physiotherapist who arrived with a chair and a portable foam wedge that really suited me. It has transformed my sitting from being uncomfortable in the Hospital, due to the chairs being too high, to something more pleasant. I started unpacking but when only half way through I knew lie-down time was essential. Bridget came later and kindly finished my unpacking. A very welcome gesture.

I'll sign off now. I have similar thoughts to my entering the Hospital. How does one behave as a convalescent? I shall see how it unfolds from my side and yet fit in with what is expected here. I have gathered already, from talking to the Director of Services, that there is a policy of freedom in the sense that I can come and go as I please as long as I let staff know that I will be absent from particular meals or will be returning home late. That suits me fine! The overall policy is I sense whatever helps the individual get well is what matters. That sounds eminently sensible.

Saturday, December 9th. 6.30 p.m.

I now have tasted a full day here. Managing the convalescent period of illness has had a Cinderella existence in health care. The convalescent centre here is probably the only one of its kind in the whole country. Some nursing homes and hospitals set aside beds or units for convalescents but that is not quite the same thing. The lack of adequate and appropriate convalescent facilities within the Health Services has been a hobby-horse of mine for years. Little thought has been given to the philosophy, general ethos and good practice required for this type of service and for the specific training of its staff. This centre offers an excellent model. The tradition behind this place goes back to 1865. The original building from that period closed five years ago and the service was then transferred to this modern purpose built unit.

The dictionary meanings of the words around convalescence are interesting. It defines convalescence as 'the gradual recovery of health and strength'. The noun convalescent refers to 'one recovering health'. The Latin etymology of the word is divided into 'con = intensive, concentrated'; and 'valescere = to be strong'. In other words it is an intensive period of time for regaining health and strength in a concentrated way.

Convalescence is thus a specialised service for people who have just left hospital. Its sole purpose is to enable people regain maximum personal autonomy. The amount of adjustment necessary will depend on the severity and type of illness undergone. Some people may have to come to terms living with a life threatening illness or with a chronic debilitating condition either for the first time or following a relapse. Others more fortunate, like myself, hope to get back to where I was before surgery and maybe even better.

The caring expertise required differs from that in hospitals or nursing homes. Care here focuses on *returning people to normality* both physically and psychologically. Starting with the physical, attention is given to four basic activities: eating, personal care, walking and resting/relaxing. The food is simple and wholesome and a reasonable choice of foods is allowed for all meals. Personal care involves becoming confident again in washing, showering and dressing oneself. Everyone is expected to walk to the dinning room for lunch and supper. Walking out of doors is encouraged and the place is blest here with beautiful gardens and a really long shrubbery walk for the more fit. Managing diminished energy levels requires rest periods; little and often is the best recipe.

I was very aware last night, for instance, that I was no longer cocooned by staff with acute care expertise, and neither was there the sophisticated gadgetry available that goes with such care. Hospitals can insidiously create dependency attitudes and behaviours. Convalescence fosters the restoration of independence. With acute hospital care becoming so high tech and with the stay in hospitals kept to the minimum necessary, centres such as this one become more essential. Without such centres an individual's return to as full health as is possible could be slowed down and may in fact never be achieved without such a service.

Now I am actually in convalescent care myself and not just talking about it! So what 'hit' me in a personal way as I endeavour to return to my own full functioning again? How did I apply the above theory to my first day? First of all I showered myself fully for the first time with no help in the wings. I was delighted about that. Beforehand, in the bed, I managed to take off both white elastic stockings. (A good tip is to use the big toe of your good leg to take off the stocking on the bad one!) After the shower I managed easily enough to get the stocking on the unoperated leg – but knew that in no way could I get it over the heel on the operated one. Bending forward too much could cause dislocation! That I foresee is the only chore I will be dependent on others for over the coming weeks.

My second achievement was my first walk out of doors. I ventured for about twenty minutes with a rest in the middle. It was a gloriously sunny morning even if cold. I imbibed the fresh air and sunshine with great delight. It was truly invigorating and I came back pleased with myself. I sense I could walk all day – obviously I can't – but am aware I can still only sit or lie in comfort for relatively short periods. Regarding food, I chose my menu list each morning with care giving thought to the iron, protein and bulk content of the foods. My 'healthy' choice must of course be balanced with what I actually like! The afternoon centred quite simply on resting.

I felt a bit of TV – Frost being interviewed after forty years of TV presenting – might add variety to end the day. One has the option here of renting a TV in your room or going to one of the two TV lounges. I chose the latter especially when I flicked through the RTE Guide and saw there were only two programmes this week that I was interested in.

Sunday, December 10th   9.0 p.m.

A good day and a full one. I have a goal to walk out of doors for longer periods each day. I had just started when misty rain began. Not being deterred by that I simply put my anorak hood up. Umbrellas are of no use when walking on two crutches. I did twenty minutes and then came back to lie on the bed for my quiet time.

At midday I set out for home. I got myself more easily into the car this second time round. I had with me my luggage – my chair wedge and raised loo seat! These items will be accompanying me everywhere over the next while. A great surge of excitement came over me as I drove towards my home. On the way I got the sudden inspiration to back into my parking place. This would ensure that on leaving I would always be able to open the car door fully – a must for getting in with a hip that is not allowed to bend very much. Car owners need to be attentive not to park too close to the drivers side of a disabled person's car space so that the door can be opened fully.

As pre-arranged Andy, my dog, was to be kept in the sunroom until I was firmly ensconced in my chair. When he was let in he sniffed around but did not come too close. He was afraid I think of the crutches. Over the six hours I was there – some of the time with people and some of the time on my own – he adjusted gradually to me while maintaining a cautious distance of the crutches as I walked around and went upstairs. I was pleased that this first encounter went well. Some of my friends are concerned that Andy, a lively eighteen month old Wicklow collie, will be too strong for me.

Apart from managing things easily around the house and helping to prepare lunch with ease, my biggest delight was my new chair. I saw this chair two years ago in a friend's house and when I sat in it I knew it was right for me. It took time to discover it's maker – a furniture store in Navan. I got mine this summer with these post-surgery days specifically in mind. I had no trace of pain or even discomfort the whole time I was in it. Chairs are the most important piece of furniture to think about following hip replacement surgery. It is essential to consider whether there is a chair in the house that is suitable for the post-surgery phase when you cannot bend your hip beyond a right angle. There is no right chair for everyone but there is a right one for each individual. I should say my new chair is a neat, high backed, padded, rocker, having the the gentlest of rocking movements.

I drove back to my base around 9.0 p.m. Being able to drive the car so soon is just wonderful since it gives great freedom of movement. I sense this will hasten my healing process.

Monday, December 11th 2.0 p.m.

It is always good to have the night over. That is the most difficult time because it is hard to stay comfortable for any length of time in one position: lying on your back. No alternatives are allowed. Sometimes it is the heels, other times your bottom, or the knee or actual hip area that are bothersome. I have never slept on my back which is true for most people. There are only ten more weeks of it! My sleep pattern has improved minimally since I came here. I decided last night that I would put the duvet under the sheet to give extra cushioning and had a cotton blanket on top. This did help.

Another crisp, sunny, December morning. I really enjoyed my walk – a full half hour this time. The grounds here must be one of the most extensive bits of land available on the outskirts of Dublin. (I wonder how long it will last before developers move in...) They are beautiful with broad stretches of fields and a stream running through. The views extend to Howth and the sea on one side and the Dublin mountains on the other. Absorbing the beauty of nature is a healer in itself. I cannot believe this day two weeks ago I was having surgery and here was I doing this relatively long walk.

My thoughts led me back to my musings about convalescent care. The setting is important and this place here has it both ways. Firstly, there is the well kept garden around the house with benches strategically placed here and there and also there are spacious rural-setting walks. Secondly there are buses into town just outside the main gate which provides easy access for visitors. All in all an idyllic location.

Tuesday, November 12th 7.0 p.m.

Briefly to recap on yesterday – an evening of 'partying' in my house for a group which I have belonged to for almost thirty years. I had hoped before the operation that I would make this date – and I did. I arrived at my home mid-afteroon and got back here just before midnight. I wasn't over-tired! Tired yes, but it led me to having the best sleep so far since surgery.

An historic day – President Clinton's visit to Dublin and a special eight-ieth birthday. The latter was celebrated this morning here in my room – number 11. A group of six of us rejoiced together with wine, cake, shar-ing, and much laughter. A happy time.

I spent the whole afternoon resting on top of my bed recuperating from last night and this morning's festivities. I did this because I felt it was the prudent thing to do rather than due to actual tiredness. I am gen-uinely surprised at my high level of energy. At no time so far have I had any sense of driving myself to do things.

I was aware after supper that I had only walked for fifteen minutes earli-er this morning. I needed more exercise and especially more fresh air. It was a windy night so I wrapped up well. It turned out to be an emotive half-hour walk down memory lane. I discovered to my amazement as I walked to the far end of this complex of many new buildings, a small little old-style country gate. I recognized it with delight. Today this remote and obviously little used passage is the only access, apart from the main road, into the St. Anthony's complex.

I was a founder member of St. Anthony's Out-patient Medical Rehabil-itation Centre way back in 1961. It was here I took up my first job as a newly qualified physiotherapist. It was a great time as well as a privilege to be involved in establishing this exciting new health service – the first of its kind in this country. A lot of euphoria that can go with pioneering was present. All kinds of emotions stirred in me as I walked around the place. It was dark and no one was around (since it an is area of out-patient services). However I was companioned by the beauty of an almost full moon which lit up the buildings and their new additions since my time as my thoughts went back to forty years ago.

Wednesday, December 13th 1.30 p.m.

I am just back from lunch. Meal times provide an opportunity to social-ize with the other convalescents. There are four sitting rooms – two with TV's, one for smokers, and one is called the library – a quieter place. People can therefore have as much or as little sociability as they wish. For some I am sure the chat is important. I enjoy meeting people at lunch and supper but find that is enough for me.

This morning I stayed on a bit longer in bed and caught up with my diary. Around 10.30 each morning a trolley goes round the rooms with mid-morning drinks. The selection is marvellous – tea, coffee, milk or Guinness! I have not opted for the black stuff yet but I gather many do.

There seemed to be a greater air of activity around the place this morn-ing due to three services that were taking place: the hairdresser, Mass, and the doctor. A local GP attends the Centre and routinely sees every new admission. My turn was today. The visit was brief and to the point. I disagreed with the doctor re suitable chairs for hip people who are small like myself. Sadly I felt permission was not given to 'agree to dis-agree'. I may be wrong in my interpretation.

I had another tremendous walk completing what I call the shrubbery walk. It took me three quarters of an hour, with as brisk walking as I could do on the crutches. It was like being out in the country – just fields. The weather was also kind – glorious sunshine.

Siesta time now and then I am off home to be with my dog. There is a de Mello group meeting there this evening so I am happy to be able to be present.

Thursday, December 14th 9.0 a.m.

I am taking to the keys earlier today as I rest on in bed. I enjoy these leisurely mornings with breakfast brought to me in bed. Breakfast has always been my favourite meal. They have delicious brown bread and I discovered yesterday the chefs bake it here daily. The Centre here seems very self-sufficient. They even have a small laundry for sheets and tow-els. No work seems to be contracted out. The catering staff also look after the little coffee shop which serves quite substantial snacks to visi-tors, or to anyone who wishes to avail of this service. I have noticed in particular how pleasant and welcoming the staff are to visitors. I have appreciated that very much..

I return now to the psychological aspects of care in a Convlescent Centre like this, as I perceive it. Illness, trauma to our bodies, is high on the list of stresses. Many people can cope with enormous difficulties such as relationship, finance, job, bereavement problems and yet can 'go under' when it comes to personal illness. As a result a consequence of illness can be the big 'D' – Depression. It is largely a reactive depression which is treatable (if noticed) but better still can be prevented if the immediate post-acute illness stage is handled well.

This 'handling' means that staff, families and the individual themselves are alert to this possibility. Alertness to symptoms of depression and then doing something about it early on can save this condition from becoming chronic. It also enables the person return quicker to their normal lifestyle. Mild or even moderate depression might not manifest itself until the third stage of convalescence – those early days at home.

Treatment might call for a mild anti-depressant. However *an earlier intervention* would be to provide a forum where the convalescent is encouraged to talk about their anxieties, fears, anger, and/or other negative feelings. When the acute stage of illness subsides, or following the receiving of a diagnosis that has life-long implications, an immediate reaction can be one of relief. Only later, when the realisation dawns that a reduced level of physical functioning might or will be a reality for the rest of their lives, can a 'low' mood set in. Support, especially in the form of listening, is what is most beneficial. Who gives this listening? It can be a relative or friend, a particular member of the care staff, or at times a professional might be necessary such as a counsellor. Care staff on the whole offer a genuine listening ear, but that can only be given in a fleeting manner since their other duties prevent the attentive and prolonged listening that may be required.

I have a chapter in my book *Falling in Love with Life, an Understanding of Ageing* titled 'Living Positively with Disablements'. In it I spell out in some detail what I call the acceptance journey. It is vitally important that people travel through the various stages of this journey so that they can come to the place of acceptance where full living can take place again. It is a journey similar to the grieving one. This acceptance road allows the 'if onlys', and the unrealistic 'when I am better' phrases, as well as feelings of self-pity, diminish until finally they are banished.

Coming to terms with the reality of our lives is never easy. T.S. Eliot says 'nature cannot bear too much reality'. Our journey towards living fully again, either with complete physical recovery, or with mild or severe limitations, takes time. The severer the residual disability the longer it will take. For example those who have had a bad stroke could take up to two years or more to come to a reasonable form of acceptance. Support, understanding, encouragement, the opening up of new possibilities, adjusting to a new and different lifestyle will necessitate the co-operation of others – especially the family. The family in turn may also need support, understanding and encouragement. If this is not immediately available it should be sought. Some persons with severe neurological difficulties will hopefully have the benefit of rehabilitation services where psychological support is included.

In a service such as convalescence I believe the psychological dimension of care should be specifically built into the whole package of care. For instance as well as the services of G.P., chiropody, and hairdresser, – already on offer here – could be added that of counsellor.

Friday, December 15th 9.0 a.m.

I spent a great deal of yesterday at home on my own. It was a good test as to how I would manage. It included getting myself lunch and tea, having a rest in my own bed (lovely). Most of all it enabled me to carry out an important milestone for myself: to take my dog for his walk in the local park. I knew I had built up the walking distance required to follow our normal park route. But getting there... I took it slowly and had the car as near as possible to the house with the car door open. Andy jumped in. I then drove close to the park gate. When I opened the car door he just ran into the park – no problem. I knew he would stay fairly close to me after that. I am very relieved that I know I can carry out this task. I cannot expect my friends to take him for daily walks much longer.

What did I learn from yesterday? – something I already know – namely that my energy levels are not yet normal. How could it be otherwise just two and a half weeks since surgery? I still marvel at and feel grateful for the fact that I am so well. I had not really envisaged beforehand that I would be as good as this at this stage.

I had a lie-on again this morning and here I am at the keys once more. Early morning and late night seem to be my best time for creative writing. I have noticed this before. Another thing I notice is my uncanny sleep pattern over the past ten days. First of all I deliberately do not settle down until nearly midnight to avoid an overly long night of problematic sleep. I sleep for a while and wake around 2 am. The bladder alarm usually goes off even though I have avoided drinking since nine. Then with difficulty I get back to sleep and wake again around five. After that I try to doze until breakfast.

During that dozy period this morning I reflected why am I still here when I now know I can manage everything at home. Two clear reasons came to mind – the meals and the better opportunities for resting. Here meals are presented to us and the food is good. Adequate and appropriate rest is probably what I most require. All domestic chores are done for you – the wash up, bedmaking, cleaning the room. If I was at home I would be doing all these things. Then over and above that when we are in our home environment we tend to potter around. I found myself yesterday doing little tasks around the house. Distractions abound too – especially mentally. For instance I was saying to myself how many more Christmas decorations will I try to put up? will I get a new carpet next year? what will I get for my tea? etc There are little of these distractions here.

The atmosphere generated in this centre is homely and peaceful. That is coupled with a quiet efficiency that is kept in the background. Last night I asked a young competent nurse why she chose to work here. Her answer was simple – because of the good atmosphere in the place. A further sign that reinforces this is that the turn-over of permanent staff, be they nurses or household, seems minimal.

I had a conversation yesterday morning with the Director of Services while she sat on the end of my bed. She is a remarkable woman, so suitable for her role and so pleasant. She tells me the place is almost full all the year round. I am not surprised. There are fifty two beds – ten of these are for VHI patients and forty two for people with medical cards. Over the Christmas and Easter periods, when there might be a slight lull, beds are offered for respite care.

Saturday, December 16th 9.0 a.m.

Since the muse seems to be more active in the morning I will try again. This largely means reflecting back on yesterday or working with some early morning reflections.

Yesterday morning I achieved a target I had set for myself – to walk along the seafront as far as the Martello Tower and back. It took exactly an hour. It was glorious – again another day of sunshine, blue skies, and that lovely winter crisp-cold air around me. I was really pleased to have done this. For three months before my operation this would have been impossible. My walking time using a stick was down to about twenty minutes. So a huge improvement!

I have another six days left here. I realise I have, so to speak, arrived at a level of physical functioning which for the next seven weeks I only have to keep up. But on the rest/relaxing side of things where am I? I know there is room for improvement on this score. I am not just talking about lying on top of the bed or relaxing in a chair more or even going to bed earlier. It may include these things but *quality* relaxation is more about inner attitudes, to our bodies, our total self, the whole of reality. I wrote in the hospital about attempting to live more fully in the present moment; being at what you are at in each moment of time. I know that is the key to quality relaxation but the practice is so difficult.

I have lived with this principle as an ideal for years. Over the last twelve months I have tried more consciously to put it into practice. Since day one of this hip replacement experience this foundational way of living has in fact happened better than before. But what a long way I have to go! So often in life I live ahead of the present moment – maybe by minutes, hours, weeks, months, or even years. If I keep doing this I can no longer be present to the present. Why? Because *I* am not *in* that moment; my conscious self is elsewhere. Hence I miss a great deal.

I think the Buddhist way of life has a lot to teach us – me anyway – on this score. They spell out, and formally attempt to live what I said previously was de Caussade's thinking when he wrote about the sacredness of the present moment. This *is* where life *really* happens. The past and the future are not the real world. I am reading at present Thich Nhat Hanh's book *The Miracle of Mindfulness*. He is a Vietnamese Buddhist monk, now seventy-eight, who was exiled from Vietnam because of the peace work he was doing in his own country. He now lives in a Buddhist monastery in the south of France called Plum Village. People come from all over the world, including recently two of my friends, to stay there and touch into this mindful way of living. Mindfulness according to Hanh, means *taking hold of our consciousness*, and then *keeping our consciousness alive* to the *present* reality.

I believe that it is only by adopting this form of living will we arrive at some level of integration – where our thoughts, feelings, sensations and activities become unified in some way. This is the path to finding *real rest* for our whole person.. Mindfulness enables us to combine together a keen sense of alertness with genuine relaxation; an ablity to hold both within the one experience. The fruit of this experience is inner peace and joy.

I have five bonus days left in this place. I see them as bonus since I nearly didn't take up my place here and even when I went I was not sure if I would stay for two weeks. During the remainder of my time I desire to renew my endeavours to live in this heightened awareness lifestyle which I embarked on the day I entered the Hospital. This way of living I now know from my own experience is what has assisted all the personal healing that has already taken place. Even more important is the certain knowing that if I continue on this path I have available to me a healing and a wholesome way of living life fully until the end of my days!

A saying of Jesus which means a lot to me is;'I have come that you may have life and have it to the full' (Jn10:10). I think it is marvellous that the Buddhist way of living can help to illuminate Jesus' message. It provides us with a practical 'how to'. We have so much to receive and give each other across the various religious divides. This is true eccumenism.

Sunday, December 17th   Gaudete Sunday   10.0 a.m.

Rejoicing Sunday and just eight days away from Christmas. The liturgy today contains the lovely reading: 'I want you to be happy; always happy in the Lord; I repeat, what I want is your happiness.... May the peace of God, which is so much greater than we can understand, guard your hearts and your thoughts in Christ Jesus' (Phil 4:4,7). The Centre here echoes that joyous sentiment since it is festive with all kinds of decorations including a tree and crib in the front hall. This morning there is Mass in the Centre so I intend to celebrate it with the people here.

As usual I rested on in bed even though I have been awake since six. Yesterday I attempted to rest *all day*. I had no visitors, did not go out anywhere, and only had two phone calls which came late in the evening. It was a *Time-Out* day and I feel the better of it. I was conscious I was being *gentle* with myself. I took no long walks either. I did walk outside briefly in the morning and again in the afternoon to get some fresh air and to explore a little bit more of the grounds. I spent a lot of time on the top of the bed and made two visits to the Oratory which is a lovely quiet place in the day time. Alas during the evening sounds of the TV take over from the sitting room next door.

I read a bit – especially the Mindfulness book. I am trying in general to read more slowly. My reflections as well as activities of yesterday focused on rest. Part of achieving tranquillity is letting go the unfinished business of the past. I cannot say I have arrived at that point but I think I am on the way there. Past hurts, disappointments etc. have receded and in many instances have disappeared. Inner peace also demands letting go of anxiety which is always future-related. I think I am more ready now to receive life as it presents itself moment by moment in the present. Achieving harmony and balance in life has something to do with how we handle our anticipations of the future. If we live with genuine hope we anticipate in a more open-ended fashion which in turn enables us to be more ready for the unexpected as well as the mundane. The ideal must surely be to develop a permanent attitude of being open to and *ready for whatever comes*. Of course I do not always succeed in all of this and can become very irked and/or impatient when things do not go the right way from my perspective.

To be able to remain present in the present is the real art of human living. Put that way I have a long road yet to travel. Yesterday I dipped in and out of this reality literally only for seconds. Tip of the iceberg stuff....

I was aware, today being the 17th December, that it is the time the great 'O' antiphons are sung at Vespers from now until Christmas. Today's one is 'O Wisdom'. I remember in my Rome days going all the way over to the Benedictine Monastery of San Anselmo one Advent to hear this intoned. The emotion expressed in the liturgy coming up to Christmas is always I find very beautiful. It captures a sense of wonder, delight, and intense longing....

Monday, December 18th   11.0 a.m.

A week to Christmas and a few days until I leave here. It could be easy to settle down in such a comfortable spot. Yet in another sense I know I am almost ready to go. I think two weeks is about right as the set time for convalescence for most people. The VHI must think the same because that is what they cover people for when convalescence is ordered by the doctor.

A point arose yesterday at our meal conversation. A new arrival (post-hip replacement) wondered what she should be doing – how much resting, walking, where to walk etc. I gently tried to suggest to her that she had been discharged from the hospital by her doctor and that the people here would not be telling her what to do. She had received the guidelines in hospital – it is now up to her to put these in practice in ways she finds appropriate. It was a good example to me of how dependency insiduously can develop during hospitalisation. Convalescence is quite different. It is about taking back personal responsibility for the recovering of our own health. I think it is a time when we tell ourselves what to do; start having a little discipline about a regime that progresses in stages each day. Staff here are there to encourage and support, but not to set out a plan for people.

I have not spoken about my hip for a while. The reason must be that it no longer bothers me (except in bed and when sitting for too long). When I walk it simply does not enter my consciousness any more. I now have to bring my consciousness deliberately to bear on it! It must be a couple of years since that has happened. I am though conscious of the unoperated leg. I definitely now have to declare it as my bad leg!

Another slight problem which I suppose is common to everyone is that the skin on both legs has got so dry. This I presume is due to the elastic stockings. The last two days I have tried to remedy this by creaming them with royal jelly. I leave it on for a couple of hours before putting the stockings back on again. I realize how fortunate I am it is winter time; the stockings must be very uncomfortable in summer heat.

I had the uplift this morning of a hairdo! My hairdresser kindly offered to give me a blow-dry after the operation. It is three weeks since I washed it so it was about time. I also wanted it done today because I have two parties in a row . She came here and it was done in ten minutes. Thank you. Chris.

Tuesday, 19th December Midday.

I survived last night's party well and was able to enjoy it thoroughly. Wine, food, good company, Santa's sack of gifts, harp and guitar solos plus amusing turns, made up the evening. I drove myself there and back returning at almost midnight and was welcomed by the night nurse with a lovely smile.

Today I plan to rest on top of the bed most of the day to be ready for tonight's marathon!

Yesterday on my way to lunch I saw a poor lady in a wheelchair feeling desperately unwell. Not everyone has convalescence as easy as myself. Some patients have had eye surgery and several have had open-heart surgery. The latter naturally tend to be nervous about themselves and need a lot of encouragement to risk doing that little bit more everyday. Some too, I have discovered, may be put on new medication which requires careful monitoring, like blood pressure checks several times a day. This is one reason why the ratio of nurses to care staff needs to be higher than in nursing homes.

Dreadful day weatherwise. It was the first time I had to use my raincoat to go out. I was glad I had it. The miserable day does not reflect my mood. I continue to consciously live with a sense of wellness and *aliveness*. My gratitude equally continues for this being so. Friday – my discharge date – comes closer. I further prepared myself for it yesterday afternoon by walking from my house to the local shops and then to doing some business at the bank. But generally it is wind-down time over the next two days.

Wednesday, December 20th 11.0 a.m.

The morning after the night before! I am still in bed not having showered or dressed yet. The marathon turned out to be a great occasion. Before going out I told my table companions what I was doing. One lady said I was mad, and one of the men said 'you're great!'. Typical opposite responses we sometimes get to what we do in life. Each one is entitled to their view. Hopefully as we move on in life we are less coloured by what people say or think, or what we think people are saying and thinking. Growth in inner freedom is one of the qualities I would most want for myself and others as we move on in years.

Well last night's happening was a continuation of the 80th birthday celebrations. It had been planned for some time. Seven of us went to the Old Dublin restaurant for a delightful meal. I was picked up this time and chauffeured to the place. The meal was leisurely, the food and wine good, the service friendly and the company excellent. I arrived with my paraphernalia of two wedge cushions and my loo seat. I was touched by the staff who produced a relatively low sized, carvery type, arm chair for me – it was just perfect so I sat in comfort for the entire meal.

That was just stage one of the evening. We left then for the Gaiety Theatre for the Sing-a-long *Sound of Music* which started at 11pm! (remember I am still the convalescent!). It was hilarious. I suppose it took me and some of our group a few minutes to get into the atmosphere and literally the swing of things. Once I was drawn into the event – the singing, the actions, and the general mood of the audience – it was great. I forgot about sitting except once when I went for a short walk to stretch the legs. I had an aisle seat. Again the two wedges fitted perfectly into the theatre seats – sitting on one and using the other as a back rest. The 'performance' ended just before 3am. Yet again the lost sheep was welcome back at the Centre at 3.30!

I note our identification bracelets here are different to the hospital. On it is your name; no personal number but instead the address and phone number of the Convalescent Centre. I suppose it is for the likes of me – should we get lost!

Just one full day before leaving here. This thought gives me a slightly strange feeling. It will be a month to the day when I return home on Friday. The whole experience has been significant. Not only do I go back with a new hip, but with a widened perspective on life. Yes I do think that is true. I have seen things/reality with different, with *fresh eyes*. Overall it has been a *good* experience for me.

I don't think I have ever before taken time-out for myself in such an intensely holistic way. Years ago I made a thirty-day retreat. That was different but it did lead to a change of direction in my life. I sense maybe a directional change may be the outcome of what has happened in me over the past month. It certainly has shown me that if you consciously try to enter life *as it is* in the fullest way possible – then you get a taste of life's over-flowing dimension. I do not think this has been a selfish enterprise – rather the opposite. It has helped to put me in touch with the whole of reality – the immediate environment as well as the whole universe in which we live – in a much richer way.

11pm

I went home for the afternoon and evening. I had previously planned to have two clients for counselling in the afternoon. Since I felt well enough I went ahead. It was good to start work again in this gentle way.

Thursday, December 21st The winter solstice 7.0 p.m.

The shortest day in the year. I thought of the privileged few at New-grange this morning waiting for that shaft of light. Today's sunrise in that stunning building echoes for me the words of Isaiah written in the seventh century BC: 'The people that walked in darkness has seen a great light; on those who live in a land of deep shadow a light has shone.' (9:1) The light /darkness theme is familiar to us all since it touches all our lives both externally and internally. The dark patches are, I believe, made easier when the light of revelation shines. In my quiet time today I went back again to Ps 16 and the line 'you will reveal the path of life to me' (11) struck a chord as I prepare to leave here tomorrow. I note in myself the desire at least to try and walk that path of *life* and not succumb to those attitudes, feelings and behaviours that have a deadening effect.

This morning for two whole hours I was sucked into Pat Kenny's radio show on Glenstal Abbey. The personal interviews with several of the monks were really interesting. I was struck by the natural way they as monks live the Benedictine way of life in modern Ireland. I sensed over-all that there was no incongruity/tension between their monastic life-style, with its attempt to publicly connect with God, while at the same time they remain grounded in our overly materialistic world. Their con-tribution towards helping transform our existing culture through the many artistic, agricultural, scholarly and other gifts of the members of the community struck me as something very wholesome.

My last evening here. I am ready for home yet at the same time I sense the next stage is going to be a bigger step down than that between hospi-tal and convalescence. Settling into a routine where the pace is balanced may not be that easy. Also the wonderful contact and support I have had from friends will obviously lessen. The pattern of living from my hip point of view cannot alter much until I have my review with my surgeon exactly a month away. Again I shall see – but for now: LIVE IN THE PRESENT!

STAGE THREE: HOME – THE FIRST TWO WEEKS

Saturday, December 23rd   2.0 p.m.

I intend to record the experience of these first two weeks at home but not necessarily on a daily basis.

I left the Convalescent Centre yesterday morning and drove home. On arrival the first hurdle was getting my bag from the car into my house. It was heavy. I hailed a walker passing by my house to do the needful and it was kindly done. Most other things I hope to be able to do on my own. Time will tell.

I now have my first night over me. It is a big transition, from having a fleet of people to call on by the simple press of a bell, to having no one around. Being independent at home when living alone requires planning manoeuvres beforehand and taking time doing each task. Then I feel I will get there. The important thing is to have no deadlines and even if the phone rings to take my time in reaching it. Those in the know will wait that bit longer, I hope.

My sitting-room looks Christmassy. I was given the lovely gift of a fibre-optic tree which changes its coloured lighting every few seconds in a nice gentle way. I have an abundance of cards which surprises me as some of the senders had already given a 'get-well' one two weeks ago. Most generous.

My walk in the park with my dog, both yesterday and again this morning went well. I hope this continues.

Today I sense is a kind of day when the pause button has been pushed in. I want it that way and will release it tomorrow – Christmas Eve. I have bits of reading – my novel and a periodical – to finish. I also need to finish my unpacking which is tedious. Two crutches slow you down when you are trying to get everything back into its rightful place – some items belong downstairs and others up stairs. It is now siesta time. So I must keep my promise to myself on that one.

Tuesday, December 26th Noon

Christmas has been and gone. I was delighted to be able to enter into my usual Christmas Eve and Christmas Day happenings with nil interference from my new hip. A tradition in our family is to gather in my home on Christmas Eve evening for the vigil celebrations of Christmas. Our traditional family supper on this occasion consists of potato soup and bread followed by mince pies. Every family has its own unique traditions and rituals at Christmas – this is one of ours.

Christmas Day morning was spent quietly on my own which I always like. Then comes time for friends and in the late afternoon I drove to my sister's where the family gathers for the Christmas dinner. Our numbers this year were down to five. Not so many years ago we were eighteen; now most of the family live outside the country.

This home part of convalescing is progressing nicely. Everything takes longer than usual, dressing, washing, getting meals etc. I was determined to continue the practice of having breakfast in bed followed by a lie on. To do this I have a small kettle upstairs and what I need on a tray. All I have to bring up the night before is some brown bread. It has worked well.

My dog gets me out of bed around 10.30 am (he has a great bladder!). These mornings I've needed to dress up well because of the cold – again that takes time. But the walks have been good and benefited both of us. In a two-bedroomed house there are no corridors for walking like in the Hospital or Convalescent Centre so I need this walk for my new hip as well as to keep up a general level of fitness.

A slight difficulty is that it takes me a bit longer to get to the phone. Not everyone lets it ring long enough. I do have a cordless one but then two nights I forgot to recharge it. It's hard to think of everything! I find it frustrating at times when I drop things. The crutches are great for picking up larger objects but only the pick-up stick does for small things. At times I find it upstairs when I need it downstairs and vice-versa.

My mood is good. But these days after Christmas are strange days – for a lot of people? Nothing much happens and for me anyway the parties all take place before Christmas. The one thing I do miss is going down to Shekina, my Wicklow Garden. I usually go for the day on Stephens' Day. That will have to wait a little longer when I feel able for an hour's drive. I am almost at that point.

Thursday, 28th December Midday

Snow on the ground this morning! An obstacle to overcome on my park walk. I first carefully ventured out with a kettle of lukewarm water to remove the snow from my car. When in the park I opted to walk on the grass rather than the paths which were slippy. I returned to base all in one piece!

Last night I went out to dinner in a friend's house. I decided not to bring my raised loo seat. I thought I might last but didn't and did a 'hovering' type job. It was not that easy and probably not the wisest of moves! There are daily little reminders of being in a 'not-yet' state. I am being careful of manoeuvres which are definitely not on.

Sunday, 31st December 1.0 p.m.

The last day of the year. Memories of the excitement of last year's New Years Eve. I spent most of it from early morning onwards with my globe in front of me watching Sky News as the new millennium began in the different parts of the world. It was an awesome time. This year we enter the first year of the third millennium and then the year after we have the Euro!

The previous three days there had been snow and ice to battle with on my walks in the park. Then this morning high winds and rain! If it were not for my dog I might just have stayed indoors these last four days. I appreciate Andy's making me go out into the challenging elements. I really enjoyed the outings once I got myself out of doors. The heavy rain this morning called for the wellies – especially necessary to protect my elastic stockings. Getting in and out of these required some ingenuity but I managed. There are ways around doing so many tasks. 'Necessity is the mother of invention' is a real truism.

Sleep is gradually improving. Last night I had five hours without any wakening. That is the best so far.

Apart from having visitors and visiting I have done some reading. Over the past decade or so I have noticed that just when I have nothing I particularly want to read then a book that grabs my attention comes across my path. I got two books this Christmas and the one I am reading is *Mad Crazy Love* by Mark Hederman, a monk at Glenstal. In the pre-

Christmas Radio Programme on Glenstal (already referred to) I heard Mark Hederman speak about the world of 'desires'. I felt I wanted to hear more... And a few days later this book landed in my lap! It is all about that topic. He speaks of the difference between human needs and desires. I appreciate this distinction yet I feel when it comes to attempting to care for one of our four basic human needs – the spiritual – it is precisely by attending to our desires that we answer the basic needs of the human spirit. This spiritual part of all make-up lies firmly within each person's human experience. In general the needs of the spirit are the ones least thought about and as a consequence they are the dimension of the human person most poorly attended to.

To be human is to have desires. Even the atheist has a spiritual life, namely a life of desires. Such desires reveal themselves in the inner restlessness we experience; a restlessness which incessantly seeks for the 'more' in human living. We are never fully satisfied except maybe for transient moments. When we do listen and attend to our desires a bit more we experience our true self at a deeper level and this can lead to a sense of personal flourishing. The last chapter of my book *Falling in Love with Life* titled 'Ageing in Wisdom, Hope and Joy' refers to the last third of life as a time for *flourishing*.

This period of life is more likely to offer opportunities for this flourishing to occur. It is a time when we move beyond the functional way of living, so characteristic of the middle years with rearing the family and earning a living being the central focus, to orientating ourselves in the direction of our heart's desires. These desires are more likely to find a level of fulfilment when we endeavour to become human beings rather than human doings. The activities we do embrace can assist our spirit life enormously and each person has to discover what works for them. Such discernment is not easy since our deepest desires are unlikely to surface without honest searching. A sense of flourishing, or liberation of the human spirit, could for instance be furthered by: greater contact with the arts (by appreciation or actually participating in artistic activity), study, ecological endeavours, religious/spiritual pursuits, deepening long-term relationships or fostering new ones, voluntary work (where we reach out to others) etc.

Tuesday, January 2nd 6.0 p.m.

Yesterday – five weeks to the day since my operation – I reached a milestone. I drove on my own to my cottage in Wicklow, an hour's drive away. It was real joy to be there and to find everything in the garden in order after the severe weather. The reasonable weather forecast for New Year's Day was what made me decide to go. I knew I could do nothing in the garden just yet but it was simply good to be there for a few hours. I was tired when I got back but it was a natural kind of tiredness.

Today too I did that bit more. I ventured on the bus into town to do some shopping. It was an interesting experience manoeuvring on and off the bus, as well as noting people's reactions. On the whole people did notice, (my clumsiness I am sure), and were considerate, including the bus driver who did not move on until I was firmly in my seat. On my return I waited at a stop with a shelter and a seat – just made for 'hippies' – high enough and sloping forward. Ideal!

As many of the general public are today returning to normality after a ten day Christmas break, so too I sense I am returning to more normal living as I enter my sixth week post operation. I am having clients starting from tomorrow and my first group meeting is tonight. I feel I am ready now for this. Last week I would have been pushing myself if I attempted to do what I did these last two days.

Friday, 5th January Midday

My six weeks since entering the Clinic ends today. I must say I have been delighted with my progress and how well I feel. Many have actually commented on how well I look. (It makes me wonder what I actually did look like before surgery!).

Over the past two days I am largely down to one crutch within the house. I am very particular though *not to take a single step* without that crutch – for fear of breaking the wires. Outside the house and especially on my walks I use the two. The other activity I have just accomplished is taking a shower at home. Before surgery I had a grab rail put in on the wall alongside the bath and it is this that makes showering both possible and safe. I needed the shower most of all to wash my hair. I also have come to the end of my iron tablets so hopefully my blood is back to near normal.

Friday seven weeks ago I entered hospital and started this diary that very day. Now as I return to more ordinary living again I feel it is appropriate to finish it at this point. Two key insights surfaced in me when I ended stage one and two of this experience. At the end of the first stage it was: SLOW DOWN! and at stage two: LIVE IN THE PRESENT! A third wisdom saying now strikes me as personally important as I terminate stage three and look forward to the future: APPRECIATE THE PRECIOUSNESS OF ORDINARY EVERYDAY LIVING. The three sayings inter-relate well and together they offer a valuable frame of reference for living – for myself I should say.

Useful objects to think about before hip replacement surgery.

Pick-up Stick. It is useful to have while in the hospital especially if you want to dress while in there

Shoes. Slip on variety that require no manual help to get on. A slight heel can be helpful

Nightdresses. Short ones are best

Raincoat with hood For outdoor walks in convalescent period.

Shower – walk-in variety for when you get home is the ideal. It is helpful to place a grab rail on wall alongside the bath for when you feel confident to use a shower in a bath.

Raised toilet seat These can be purchased through the hospital or maybe you can borrow from a friend who has one

A hand grip might be necessary beside the toilet.

A suitable chair – one high enough not to bend your hip to a right angle when sitting and with arms.

A chair wedge These foam wedges can be useful for the car and for ordinary sitting. They can be purchased through the hospital or convalescent centre.

A cordless phone is useful when you get home.

An automatic car – is the ideal for those (especially with left hips) who want to drive immediately after their hospital stay – provided your surgeon approves.

APPENDIX TWO

Outline of hospital routine following hip replacement surgery
(This will vary slightly depending on the surgeon)

Day One: Operation

Day Two: Exercises in bed. Drip taken down

Day Three: Drains taken out. Stand out of bed. Short walk in room in a.m. and p.m. on frame.

Day Four: Walk twice daily on corridor. Allowed to use the toilet and to wash at the sink

Day Five: Sitting out for two fifteen minute periods. Three walks and longer distances

Day Six: Sitting for longer periods. Unsupervised walking four times daily

Day Seven: Shower. (I dressed from that day on)

Day Eight: Walking with crutches. Go to Physiotherapy Department for exercises

Day Nine: Do the stairs

Day Ten: Check day – i.e. blood tests, x-ray, nuclear pulmonary scan

Day Eleven: Physiotherapy talk on the do's and don'ts post hip replacement surgery

Day Twelve: Stiches removed. Discharged

Statistics for Total Hip Replacements in Ireland for 1999

General Hospitals   **2784**
(Cappagh Hospital had the largest number of cases – 787. This
figure includes both public and private patients. This is also true of
the General Hospitals around the country who do total hip replacements.)

Four Private Hospitals in Dublin City .   **702**
(Mount Carmel, Blackrock Clinic, Mater Private, Bon Secours)

Total   3486

APPENDIX FOUR

Books referred to in the Diary

The Bible, Jerusalem Bible trans. (Darton, Longman and Todd 1966).

The Enneagram, Beesin, Nogosek, O'Leary (Dimension Books Inc. 1984).
There are many other books on the Enneagram by different authors.

Sadhana, A. de Mello, (Anand Press 1985).

Awareness, A. de Mello, (Fount, Harper and Collins 1990).
Other de Mello books include *Wellsprings, Song of the Bird, One Minute Wisdom, Prayer of the Frog.*

Abandonment to Divine Providence, J.P. de Caussade (Image 1975).

The Sacrament of the Present Moment, J.P. de Caussade, (Doubleday 1996).

Deep River, S. Endo (Sceptre 1994).

The Little Prince, A. de Saint-Exupery (Pan Books 1974)

The Miracle of Mindfulness, Thich Nhat Hanh (Rider 1991) .

Manikon Eros, Mad, Crazy Love, M. Hederman (Veritas, 2000)

Periodicals

The Tablet, ed. J Wilkins (London) A weekly periodical

The Furrow, ed. R Drury, (Maynooth) A monthly periodical